Anonymous

Club Cameos

Portraits of the Day

Anonymous

Club Cameos
Portraits of the Day

ISBN/EAN: 9783744679268

Printed in Europe, USA, Canada, Australia, Japan

Cover: Foto ©ninafisch / pixelio.de

More available books at **www.hansebooks.com**

CLUB CAMEOS:

PORTRAITS OF THE DAY.

'Quemvis media elige turba;
Aut ob avaritiam, aut misera ambitione laborat.'
HORACE, *Satires*, lib. i. iv.

WITH SIXTY-TWO ILLUSTRATIONS BY RUPERT BROWNE.

LONDON:
SAMPSON LOW, MARSTON, SEARLE, & RIVINGTON,
CROWN BUILDINGS, 188 FLEET STREET.
1879.

[All rights reserved.]

CONTENTS.

		PAGE
I.	THE HOUSE	3
II.	THE PRIVATE SECRETARY	29
III.	THE GUARDSMAN	51
IV.	PATRIOTISM	75
V.	LETTERS	97
VI.	THE CLUB	125
VII.	M. F. H.	151
VIII.	CULTURE	177
IX.	FINANCE	201
X.	WITS	221
XI.	THE OLD SCHOOL	247
XII.	SOCIAL AMBITION	269
XIII.	BOHEMIA	291
XIV.	A PARASITE	313
XV.	AGITATION	337

THE HOUSE.

THE HOUSE.

WITHIN the last two generations a revolution, bloodless, gradual, and unobtrusive, but none the less radical and subversive, has been working within our midst. Silently, yet surely, the invading forces of Wealth and Competition have marched into the once exclusive territory of Privilege, and dethroned her from her narrow and haughty position. We have had the age of the feudal system, when knightly deeds were the passport to distinction; we have had the age of superstition, when the priesthood was supreme; we have had the intellectual age, when literary activity was the highway to fame; we have had the dissipated age, when gallantry was the only education of the satellites of fashion; and now in this nineteenth century we have, in all its glory, ostentation, power, and vulgarity, the Age of Money:

> 'omnis enim res,
> Virtus, fama, decus, divina humanaque, pulchris
> Divitiis parent; quas qui contraxerit, ille
> Clarus erit, fortis, justus—Sapiensne? Etiam! et rex,
> Et quicquid volet.'

Disguise it as we may, wealth is the governing force in

our social system. Birth has its limits, intellect is fettered by restrictions; ready money alone amongst us can walk erect straight on to its goal, and be master of all it surveys. What barrier opposes it? It surmounts its newly-found escutcheon with a coronet, and takes its seat amongst the Howards and the Talbots of the House of Lords. It is sworn of the Privy Council and is enrolled in the Cabinet. It takes the oath before the Speaker, and is the representative of wealthy shires and important boroughs. It buys up lands, castles, halls, and manor-houses; it is put into the commission of the peace, wears the scarlet and silver of the deputy-lieutenant and the gorgeous uniform of the yeomanry, and constitutes itself an important section of the landed gentry. It contracts brilliant marriages; it enters, and sometimes leads, society; its sons officer the crack regiments; its daughters command the matrimonial market; in short, there is no boundary to its ambition, no confine to its power. Instead of the pedigree-chart we have substituted the banker's-book.

There was a time, however, and that not very long ago, when wealth and social position did not necessarily go hand in hand together. Birth had its sphere and bullion its own circle. Commerce drew its votaries from its own set, leaving the higher things in life to its betters. An unbridged gulf stood between the moneyed proletarian and the haughty aristocrat. It was right that the aristocrat should dance at Almack's, should play his rubber at White's, should command his troop in the Blues or the First Life Guards, should be returned for a close borough, and burden the state with his sinecures.

It was his right, his due, the necessary consequences that ancient lineage entailed. As for the City man, he had his ambition and settled career: let him become a director of the East India Company or the Bank of

England, a member of the Court of Aldermen, Lord Mayor, the warden of a company, or anything that the commercial classes might aspire after; but forbid it, Heaven, that his vulgar figure should obtrude itself into the coteries of society, that his plebeian hands should shuffle the cards in an exclusive club, that his sons should be attached to embassies or obtain commissions in crack regiments, that he should oust the landed gentry from the soil, and deem himself the equal of men whose ancestry dated back to the Conquest!

Such were the views—views as old as the days of Aristotle and of Plato—that society held as to the position of commerce until the beginning of this century. Trade was ignoble; the only occupations fit for 'a gentleman' were arms, diplomacy, the Bar, and the Church. But such narrow teaching exists no more. Commerce, with its splendid fortunes, its exciting career, its rapid profits, has cast the professions into the shade, and counts among its followers some of the best blood in the land. What is the income of a leading barrister, of a renowned physician, of a bishop, or an ambassador, or a statesman, when compared with the colossal profits of a great tea-broker, corn-merchant, brewer, distiller, warehouseman, stockbroker, or of that omnivorous creature the general merchant? No wonder that the sons of peers gladly accept partnerships in good firms, that dandies go on 'Change, and that the voice of Fashion declares that 'there is nothing like trade nowadays.' Privilege, with its airs and graces, its comfort

and convenience, its patronage and its injustice, is dead and buried, and over its newly-raised mausoleum Capital and Competition dance in jubilant triumph.

I am led to make these reflections whenever I have the pleasure of meeting my friend Mr. Angus McWelder, the wealthy iron-master east of the Clyde, and member for the Forge Burghs. In none of our institutions has Reform been more busy with its abolitions and innovations than with the House of Commons. Before the measures of 1832 and 1867 became law, a young man of good blood or of great ability could take his seat upon the green benches of the Lower House as the nominee of some powerful peer or opulent squire, without being put to the expense of a single farthing. In this easy fashion the second Pitt, Canning, and Macaulay entered the House of Commons. But at the present day, thanks to Reform Bills and the establishment of Election judges, to become a member of Parliament (save in certain exceptional cases, where brilliant talent or a hereditary name specially recommends itself to a constituency) requires money, and in many instances money alone. What chance has the most glib barrister or the most clever adventurer against some local plutocrat who builds a new wing to the town hospital, erects almshouses for the poor, subscribes liberally to the racecourse, gives cups at regatta meetings, and on all occasions drops his money as freely perhaps as he does his *h*'s? What chance has an unknown new-comer, with a few hundreds advanced to him out of the funds of the political committee of his club, against the man of capital who has been 'nursing' the borough for years in the expectation of a vacancy, and who, in spite of bribery and corruption clauses, lets the inhabitants of the town know perfectly well that if they stand by him he will be their friend, spend his money amongst them, look after their local interests, and assist them in all their urban improvements?

Two things are now requisite to obtain a seat in Parliament—money and a long courtship to the shire or borough selected by the candidate. The consequence is that these conditions cause the House of Commons of the present day to be a somewhat dull assembly; its members having taken to politics late in life, there is an absence of that youthful talent which made the House bright with its keen wit in the 'good old times' of close boroughs and nomination boroughs.

From what I hear of Mr. McWelder, he is not calculated, either by his wit or his eloquence, to enliven the character of the debates. He is interested in but one subject—the sewage question; and as the word 'manure,' which he calls, by the way, 'manyer,' enters largely into the composition of his speeches, the wags have christened him 'Old Guano.' No matter what may be before the House—the Estimates, affairs in the East, the repair of a turret-ship, Church reform, and the like—as sure as McWelder rises to speak, so sure will the current of his eloquence finally flow into the drainage question, until cries of 'Order, order!' 'Question!' and a friendly tug at his coat-tails from his nearest neighbour brings him down from the lofty height of his subject to his seat. The appearance of McWelder is not in his favour. His face is red and

rough like a Highland steer, and crowned with light sandy hair which is turning gray at the roots. His eyes are small, and their expression marred by a most diabolical squint, caused apparently by a constant examination of a great wart which nestles closely at the side of his fleshy and flexible nose. His chest and barrel are huge and tremulous, and supported by short sturdy legs as bandy as the timbers of a sugar-cask. He speaks a language intelligible, I believe, to the members of his family, but which requires great care and attention on the part of the stranger to master. At times when excited upon his favourite topic, or indignant with one of the morning-room waiters because the *Scotsman* has been mislaid or the *Glasgow Herald* has not arrived, I am fearful lest his burrs and his brogue should force the roof off his mouth.

Like many men whose appearance is somewhat repelling, he is the essence of kindliness. The nut is coarse and shaggy, but the kernel is sweet and tender. When you know him he talks simply of himself, and owns with pride that he began life by trundling a wheelbarrow in one of his own quarries. On most Wednesdays and Saturdays he engages the largest table in the strangers' dining-room of the Caravanserai, and feasts his constituents, men as red, as unwieldy, and as loud and singsong in their talk as himself, and who sit far into the night over their wassail of 'whusky' in the smoking-room. Next to telling a very long story, always about Scotland and Scotchmen, which is simply incomprehensible from its want of point and constant imitation of dialect to any one not hailing from the banks of the Clyde, the delight of McWelder is to reproduce before any audience that will attend to him, in his own peculiar language, the speeches that were made the night before by the more important members of either House. To listen to my friend you would imagine that he was on the most intimate terms with every member of the Government and of the Opposition, for in conversation he calls them all by their Christian names. If the Earl of Beaconsfield has laid before their lordships in the Upper House some important disclosures as to the state of foreign affairs during a season of grave crisis, McWelder innocently remarks as he snorts over the *Times* to me or to some one else of his acquaintance, 'Ye should have hair-r-r-r-r-d Benjamin in the Lor-r-rds last nicht; it wus jist pair-r-r-fect.' Should the name of the Chancellor of the Exchequer crop up, it is McWelder's opinion 'that Stafford is doing vara weel in the Hoose, leddie; dinna fash yersel, he can hold his ain against William.' When he alludes to the most noble the leader of the Opposition, or to the Right Honourable the Speaker, he speaks of those august persons in so familiar a manner that you might imagine he was a blood relation of the family. No matter who the man is whose life or whose character is being discussed, whether he be a Cabinet Minister or a judge or an ambassador or a bishop, provided that he at least be a somebody, McWelder will always make some casual remark about him, and designate him by his Christian name. Why he does this no one knows, for he is the last man to give himself airs and assume swagger. How he remembers the Christian names of all the great people he so familiarly alludes to is also a puzzle to me. Whisky must be very conducive to a good memory.

Until I became more intimately acquainted with McWelder, an acquaintance since cemented by a diligent study of Sir Walter Scott and the glossary to Burns's poems, it was a matter of wonder to me why he should have embraced a parliamentary career. He did not want a baronetcy; he had no social aspirations; his education, to put it kindly, was imperfect; he had no strong political opinions; he had no special grievances to air. Why, therefore, should an uncouth untutored man, who was the head of a most important manufacturing industry, give up his valuable time, neglect his business, and incur a grave expenditure to embark upon a career for which he was both socially and intellectually unfitted? The question is a reasonable one; let me therefore answer it from information that I afterwards received. Mr. McWelder, as soon as Fortune began to smile upon him, and iron to claim him for its own, took unto himself a wife, the daughter of a large manufacturer at

Galashiels. For several years their married life kept the even tenor of its way. McWelder, engrossed by his commercial operations, had very little time for anything else, and what leisure fell to him was spent in improving the magnificent estate he had lately purchased from a Scotch peer, whose descent was as rapid as McWelder's ascent. As Mrs. McWelder annually for some seven years presented her lord and iron-master with pledges of her love with the most painful punctuality, she naturally had little opportunity for idleness. When she wanted change of air, she was delighted with a tour in the Highlands, or with the shooting-box on her husband's moors; and when she thought a little society would do her good, she and her husband took a house in Edinburgh for the winter. Neither their thoughts nor their ambition went beyond their being happy and useful in the position that Providence had placed them. Fond of her husband and of her children, Mrs. McWelder's life was one most equal and contented. But the serpent was on the trail to poison her with its venom.

It so happened that a Mr. McMashem of Ayr, a wealthy brewer and intimate friend of McWelder's, was returned to Parliament for Vatlivat. Mrs. McMashem now lorded it over poor Mrs. McWelder, though they had been at school together and had learnt the Westminster Catechism together, to an extent not to be borne by human endurance. She took the *pas* of her on every occasion. She laughed at the people of Glasgow; she ridiculed the clerical and legal society of Edinburgh; she took her children from a Scotch boarding-school and sent them to Rugby; she quitted the Free Church and became an Episcopalian; she affected to talk English; and in short, she pooh-poohed everything and everybody about her. 'There was only one place to live in, and that was London,' she said over and over again to Mrs. McWelder. Indeed, the good lady brewed mischief as her husband brewed beer.

The die was cast. Nothing would now satisfy Mrs. McWelder but that her husband should enter Parliament, and she be on a footing of equality with that 'ojous' Mrs. McMashem. Need I say that when a lady takes anything very violently into her head nothing on the earth beneath or in the waters under the earth will prevent her from attaining her object? McWelder felt that if his life was to be bearable he must submit to his wife's wishes. He was somewhat disturbed in his mind as to which political party he should attach himself. Should he be a R*aa*dical, or should he be a Cons*air*vative? His impartial wife came to his rescue. 'Ah, Angus, dinna fash yersel aboot political opeenions; jist enter the

Hoose o' Commons for ainy toon that'll tak ye! Ye can think of opeenions aifter!' The prospect of an immediate vacancy in the Forge Burghs—which had been Tory since Sheriffmuir—decided McWelder to enrol himself in the ranks of the 'Consairvative' party. He hurried up to London, saw the political agent, and was interrupted in an eloquent speech upon the purity and fidelity of his political principles by the practical question, What was he prepared to spend? It was the old story of 'them as pays my rent has my vote.' The Forge Burghs were commercially ambitious: they wanted a new dock; they wanted a new pier, a good quay, warehouses, harbour drainage, a junction with the North British Railway, and a few other moderate requests. The man who helped them the most in carrying out their intentions was sure of being returned. McWelder came down with his hundreds like a man, and soon caused his opponent—a respectable Edinburgh advocate, who could talk a horse's hind leg off upon such questions as education, the Established Church, the law of hypothec, Scotch currency, &c., but whose purse was more slenderly stocked than his head—to desist from canvassing. For the last five years the great iron-master has represented the Forge Burghs.

It is said that as soon as a man becomes acclimatised to the peculiar atmosphere of the House of Commons he cares to breathe no other air. This is the case with McWelder. Outside St. Stephen's all is now a blank and devoid of interest to him. His eldest son carries on the business, and his wife, thanks to ministerial receptions

and to her hospitalities at the big house in Cromwell-road, is getting on in London society, and McWelder is left much to his own devices. He is always at Westminster, and is ever to be depended upon to make up a House; for when not in the presence of the Speaker or the Chairman of Committees, he is sure to be in the smoking-room or in the little apartment sacred to the genial Sergeant-at-Arms. He speaks constantly; but as no one listens to him, he takes his revenge by writing out his speeches (with casual interpolations of 'cheers,' 'loud cheers,' 'hear, hear,' and 'laughter') and sending them to his subsidised organ, the *Forge Daily Blower*. He serves on committees, and it has fallen to my lot occasionally to hear him examine a witness; one of the clerks has at last been appointed as an interpreter.

Nothing he more delights in than being attentive to such ladies as he ushers into their latticed gallery. How he hands them their tea! how he informs them of the customs of the House! how he points out all the distinguished members, talking of them of course as William and Robert and John and Henry! how polite, how garrulous, how egotistic he is! I fancy he does not tell Mrs. McWelder the names of *all* the ladies he puts down in the book. On an important night, when the entrance to the lobby is thronged with spectators anxious to obtain admission into the House, how slowly, how majestically he passes the policemen and runs the gauntlet of inquiring eyes! Surely that bent figure, that thoughtful brow, that absorbed air can belong to none other than a Cabinet Minister full of the grave information he is about to lay before Parliament! How he stands about the lobby, with that peculiar House-of-Commons air which is so different from every other form of swagger, or unites himself to little groups of members, or walks arm-in-arm with a friend, solemn and thoughtful, as if upon his rounded shoulders all the responsibilities of the Empire rested! Yet he is no humbug. Though he thinks there is no club like the House of Commons—its chat and gossip the best, its dinners the best, its smoking-room the best, its library the best,—and that he would like to be buried in a House of Commons coffin beneath the flags of the Embankment, still he serves his constituents well. He attends to all their local requests; works at what private bills they require; never shirks them when they call upon him; dines with them; puts their names down for the Speaker's or the Strangers' Gallery; does his best to get them places in the Customs or the Revenue; patronises their sons; promises a good deal, and fulfils not a little.

McWelder is one of the shining lights of the Caravanserai (to which splendid establishment I also belong), and he uses the club very frequently. Whenever her Majesty or the Speaker holds a *levée*, he generally puts in an appearance afterwards in the smoking-room to exhibit the green and gold of his Archer's uniform. The waiters fear him, for his orders are not very intelligible to the Southern ear, and he is apt to be irritable when asked to repeat his request. He is fond of the society of young men, many of whom, I regret to say, with the insincerity of youth, eat his dinners, smoke his cigars, dance at his wife's balls, ride his horses, use

his opera-box, ask him for Speaker's orders, and then behind his back imitate his peculiarities and ridicule his kindnesses. Fortunately McWelder is not thin-skinned. He can listen unflinchingly to the derisive laughter of the House when turned against him; he can bear unmoved its offensive indifference to his speeches; chaff, innuendoes, invective, are powerless to wound him. With amusing blindness McWelder is under the impression that he is a practical statesman and a politician of a high order. The office he especially considers himself fitted for is that of President of the Local Government Board. He has lately been elected a member of the committee of the club; consequently his first duty was to make inquiry into its drainage system. Undoubtedly, as McWelder says, a special knowledge of any subject is always useful in the House of Commons; but it is doubtful to me whether my friend's 'special knowledge' is of such a nature as to bear him on its unsavoury tide to office, however humble. His seat is sure; his fortune large; his wife is avaricious after social honours; he has spent a good deal of money for 'the party:' it would not therefore surprise me if some day we should see on the panels of the gorgeous barouche that occasionally waits for McWelder outside the Caravanserai, the blood-red hand.

There must be something terribly fascinating in parliamentary life which the stranger to its existence fails to understand or sympathise with. When I see a man like McWelder not only interested in, but engrossed by, his duties, it is evident that St. Stephen's has charms which she only displays to those admitted within her circle. The social distinction that once attended upon the letters M.P. cannot be the attraction, for at the present day many of our legislators are little better than town councillors. It cannot be the prizes of the profession, for out of the six hundred and odd members how many draw salary from the Treasury? Why should a man abandon his business, give up much of his leisure, be absent from the country when it is most beautiful, live for many hours in a close atmosphere, keep late hours, have to attend to often dull and laborious work, spend his money, receive no pay, and be on terms of acquaintanceship with a vast number of people many of whom in all probability are repulsive to him, and all for the honour of being returned to Parliament? Yet, considering how every seat is competed for, there must be some powerful attraction in the green benches of the House of Commons, which we, who are not under the wand of the magician, fail to comprehend. I can understand certain men—the venal, the ambitious, the intellectually active—embracing a political career; they may win or they may lose; still the struggle is worth the effort. What I cannot understand is, why the men who constitute the majority of the House of Commons, the men who cannot hope to get anything, who do not even wish to get anything, who are mere voting-machines and Wednesday orators—I cannot understand why these should disburse large sums of money, should subject themselves to much physical labour, should swallow self-respect for a vote, should be eternally badgered, worried, and annoyed, for what to my simple gaze seems a game hardly worth the candle.

Some little time ago a friend of mine, a man whose birth and fortune render him independent of the ordinary aspirations of mankind, caught a terrible cold. He was put to bed; a blazing fire was all aglow in the room; the sudorific he had taken was agreeably acting; a sense of comfort and relief tingled through his frame; quiet and contented, he was immersed in the pages of *Le Nabab*. Suddenly his door-bell was rung, a messenger came in hot haste from 'the whip,' and he had to dress, to go out in the fog, and hurry down to the House of Commons to swell the ranks of the Government against the tactics of a mischievous Opposition. Why should he have subjected himself to this? *Que diable allait-il faire dans cette galère?* He never speaks in the House; he is pale with terror even when he has to address his constituents; he seldom serves on committees: he does not want a peerage; he is not a barrister intent upon reaching the woolsack; the House of Commons can give him nothing that he has not already; and yet session after session he submits to boredom, to late hours, to a bad atmosphere, and to numerous restrictions interfering with his comfort and his liberty.

I doubt whether McWelder, in the days when he was consolidating his iron business, worked much harder than he does now for the honour and glory of the thing. What with writing letters to his constituents, listening to their wants, their grievances, their applications, bothering the patient and long-suffering clerks of the House of Commons about the private bills he wants to introduce, serving on committees, occasionally being a member of a Royal Commission, hunting up references in *Hansard* for his speeches and replies, and putting in a constant attendance (when has his name been absent from the division list?) at the debates of the House, he never appears to have a minute to himself during the session; and what little leisure he possesses always seems occupied in dining his constituents, taking Mrs. McWelder to receptions, going to a State ball or concert, attending *levées*, and being entertained by the Speaker or by public companies. It is only very early in the morning or very late at night that his presence haunts the writing-room and smoking-room of the Caravanserai.

Even out of the session he is constantly occupied. When he is good enough in the autumn to ask me to Anvilhaugh Castle he can seldom spare time to shoot the grouse on the moors or the pheasants in his well-preserved coverts, because he has to preside at this dock committee, or that railway committee, or the pier improvements committee, or the Forge Burghs Young Men's Christian Association, or the Forge Burghs Quarry dinner, or the Masonic meetings of the Hammer Lodge, or the hundred and one other calls upon the time of a man who is both a popular and hardworking M.P. and an extensive landowner. Still McWelder is not to be pitied. He is so thoroughly wedded to his new life that were he to be unseated to-morrow no man north of the Tweed would be more miserable.

As for the fair *châtelaine* of Anvilhaugh, she has for a long time ceased to trouble herself with the McMashems of this life. A lady whose dinners are as well dressed as herself, whose dances are famous for the excellent condition of the floor and the magnificent suppers that follow, whose two daughters are supposed to have eighty thousand apiece, and who is every season increasing her social reputation, need take little notice of those she knew in the days of her obscurity. 'They are not in my set,' she says to me in excellent English, and in the tones of one who from her earliest infancy has been born in the purple, and always worn the colour. Ah, Mistress McWelder, though the Westminster Catechism may have taught you much, methinks the articles in the creed of London Society have taught you more! Weigh husband and wife in the balance, and the husband will be found to be the better and more sterling of the two. On the bede-roll of baronets you may find men more polished with the gloss of civilisation, and better educated with the lore of the schools, but not one more honourable in his dealings, more indefatigable in his labours, more honest and just, than the future Sir Angus McWelder, Bart., M.P. for the Forge Burghs.

THE PRIVATE SECRETARY.

THE PRIVATE SECRETARY.

Tact is to manner what genius is to talent. There are many people in the intellectual world who are clever, erudite, sharp, yet utterly destitute of genius; whilst in the social world the number of persons who are ambitious, plausible, and agreeable, and yet totally deficient in tact, is legion. How frequently do we hear questions asked which should be avoided, answers given which should be evaded, and subjects discussed which should never be introduced! How constantly do the scheming and the worldly wise show their hand, and thus mar their game, by a plausibility so palpable that it never deceives! How often is hate defeated by the intensity of its spite and its clumsy malevolence!

If men and women exhibited a little more tact in their walk through life, the snob would talk less of his intimacy with the great, Dives would boast less of his wealth, women would be more careful in their disparagements of each other, the jealous would pretend less to indifference, and the acrid would mingle a little more honey with their gall. We read of an ambition that overvaults itself and falls on the other side. It is quite as possible to fail from overdoing as from never attempting. A well-bred display is one thing, the ostentation of the vulgar another. To know a lord does not necessarily imply an incessant reference to the aristocracy. The possession of wealth is not always evinced by allusions to the balance at our banker's, the extent of our property, and the splendour of our establishment. To be familiar with a thing is to be silent about it; to be new to it is to be loquacious and intrusive.

The man who has been of the gentry for centuries never obtrudes his birth; but the *nouveau riche*, smarting under his social shortcomings, is always climbing up his family tree, and garrulous as to his ancestors. The Volunteer officer is always more military in his ideas than the warrior. The dissenting minister is often far more clerical in his attire than his brother of the Establishment. Whenever we see an over-precision in dress, in language, and in the surroundings of a man or woman, we may be sure that his or her introduction into the ranks of the cultivated is but recent.

As a rule, in that microcosm which we call society, it is easy to estimate the character of a man, or judge the disposition of a woman. But when tact envelops the subject in its subtle folds, criticism becomes more difficult. To detect between the fustian and the purple, the superficial and the solid, the moderate and the wealthy, when tact blinds the observer with its glamour, is an analysis often requiring the greatest social ability. Amongst minerals there are some precious stones which can be imitated so cunningly that even the professed lapidary is often deceived. In wandering through the dazzling alleys of Vanity Fair it is not always at a glance that we can separate the pearls from the paste. Tact, which is often only another form of imitation, baffles our penetration.

Take the case of Horry Fortescue, for instance. The son of a clergyman of good birth, but slender means, with no commanding talents, with no overpowering attractions as to face or figure, he has yet distanced all his compeers, and is already in possession of much that men envy and women admire. He never trespasses upon the paternal purse—Horry is a charming young man, and remembers that he has sisters—yet he never lacks funds. Though in these days money has ousted birth from the lofty and exclusive position it occupied during the *régime* of the Governing Families, there are still coteries guarded and protected by vigilant outposts, where the knavish capitalist, the vulgar borough member, the prosperous trader never intrude.

> 'Licet superbus ambules pecunia,
> Fortuna non mutat genus.'

In these well-winnowed assemblies the name of Horry frequently appears, whilst better and cleverer men are excluded. There are in his set men who have written books; there are glib barristers with an eye to Parliament who make great orations; yet none can draw up a document so clearly and succinctly as Horry, none at wedding-breakfast or other hospitality can say just what should be said, and no more, better than he. He is surrounded by men who spend hours over their personal adornment, and to whom Nature has granted considerable attractions; yet Horry, who runs up a modest bill with his tailor, and who will dress for dinner when pressed in some six minutes, is always considered by ladies to bear away the palm both as to attire and distinction. He is not a scholar, he is not even well read; and yet his conversation is agreeable; whilst the bookworm is silent and the erudite shy. He never makes an enemy; and yet all his friends are drawn from the serviceable class. He is all things to all men, and especially to women, but he has the good taste to shun the air of plausibility of the popular man of the clubs or the tame cat of the boudoirs. What his vices are we know not, for he keeps them rigidly to himself. His talk is clean and guarded; he respects the *convenances* of life; he shuns the slang of the turf and the betting-room; and without being a prig of the Mechanic's Institute type, or imitating the intense fastidiousness of the educated tradesman, speaks English like a gentleman. Hence in the eyes of the ladies he is deemed 'so nice;' whilst men,

in the vernacular they encourage, call him 'good form all round.'

It is now some seven years since Horry Fortescue came to town. After a career successful yet not brilliant at Harrow, he went up to Oxford to complete his education. He had scarcely furnished his rooms at Merton when he was summoned to town, and requested to seat himself at one of the bureaus in the Protocol Department, to which he was appointed by his Grace the Duke of Ambleside, the Lord Keeper of the Department, and who, as the Marquis of Windermere, had been a college friend of the father of young Fortescue. In these days of competitive examinations and Civil Service reorganisation, we need hardly say that the Protocol Department is one of the most envied of the public offices. It is divided, with a simplicity of arrangement which makes the men of the War Office and of Somerset House rage enviously, into two sections: the first section, with the title of Assistant Keepers of Protocols, begins at three hundred a year, rising by thirty-five-pound stages to six hundred; whilst the second section, with the rank of Keepers of Protocols, pays its officials from seven hundred to nine hundred a year. There are also various staff appointments, ranging from a thousand to fifteen hundred a year, which are given in the Department or not, according to the interest of the applicant inside, or the claims of hungry place-hunters outside.

The Protocol Department has this advantage over its fellows, that its candidates are appointed direct by the Lord Keeper, and have to endure no ordeal at the hands of the Civil Service examiners. It is one of the maxims of the Department that education is all very well, but that, where simple yet responsible duties are to be performed, to be what is termed a 'gentleman' is of far more importance. The Lord Keeper is always a peer of high degree, and the aristocratic mind shudders at the thought of seeing some young scion of the vulgar, whose only recommendation would be brains and a baptismal certificate, copying protocols or conventions at one of the comfortable oak bureaus of the Department, only perhaps to sell his information to the first newspaper which would bid for his services. We need hardly say that honour and honesty are exclusively confined to those born in the purple. The turf frauds, the card scandals, the City Company swindles, and the divorce revelations of recent date, have arisen, as we all know, entirely within the ranks of the plebeian. At least, such is the opinion of the Lord Keepers of Protocols from time immemorial. No son of the people, no hardworking Irish student, none of the geniuses from Glasgow and Aberdeen have ever yet entered the swinging dark-mahogany doors of the Department. The officials are all men with some claims to ancestry, their fathers standing well in the front of the landed gentry; a few of them bear titles of courtesy; also one or two have the shadow of the bar sinister across their escutcheon. A well-bred fashionable coterie is the Protocol Department, and such it is likely to remain until the seldom quoted New Zealander shall come to take a photograph of its ruins from the Thames Embankment.

Into this snug berth Horace Fortescue was ensconced. The young man well knew that little from the paternal estate could fall to his share, and that he would have to be dependent upon his own energies for his advancement in life. He worked hard, he was punctual in his attendance, and the result of his labours could generally be relied upon. There are those who imagine that the industry displayed in a Government office chiefly consists in reading the morning papers, receiving visits from friends, lounging from one room to the other, partaking of elaborate luncheons, with perhaps the copying a letter or the adding up of a total, supported by the stimulant of a cigarette or a cigar. No greater delusion exists. As a rule, the Civil servants of the Crown are as industrious and as hard worked as any other community; and considering the poverty of their pay and of their prospects, it speaks somewhat of their sense of honour that official treachery is almost unknown in their midst. What banker, merchant, or solicitor would intrust his clerks with the secrets that are often among the daily duties of a member of the Civil Service?

As in all other departments, there were men in the Protocol Office who came late and went away early, who idled their time, and who, whenever a diligent colleague was promoted, cursed their ill-luck, but never found fault with their industry. The keen calculating glance of Horry Fortescue soon saw through his brother officials, and speedily distinguished between the men who were to be his rivals and those from whom he had nothing to fear. His tact, his genial ways, his innate good taste, stood him in good stead during the struggle. The idlers knew he worked, but did not call him 'a smug;' the industrious saw they had a dangerous foe, but did not dislike him; on the contrary, he was rather popular. Gradually Horry began to obtain a reputation in the Department. The Keepers complimented him; the assistant-secretaries asked him to dinner; there was some talk of sending him abroad, attached to a commission to inspect boundaries.

But the goal upon which the ambition of Horry was firmly set was still as far removed as ever. He wanted to know his Grace of Ambleside. On his appointment he had been introduced to the Duke, who had hoped his father was well, said that he thought the morning was cold for the time of the year, trusted there would soon be a change in the weather, and—that was all. The old rector had asked a few great people he knew in town to be civil to his son, and Horry had exerted all his manœuvres to come across the consort of his Chief. But in vain. Her Grace was a volatile, impulsive, and somewhat stupid woman, who gave herself great airs, snubbed people or took them up, according to her fickle fancy, accepted invitations, and then at the last moment declined them, so that no dependence could be placed upon her word or her movements. Three times had Horry been asked to a crush in order to meet the Duchess, and it had pleased her Grace precisely at those three times not to put in an appearance. 'It all depends upon how she likes you at first,' said his fair friends; 'sometimes she likes certain young men for one thing, and then at other times hates them for exactly the same thing. It is all a chance.' But Horry knew perfectly well that where his own interests were concerned it would become a very difficult job for any one to hate him. Only let him have five minutes with the Duchess, and he would not fear the consequences.

As luck would have it, one night he met her Grace at a calico dance, to which she had not been invited, but to which she suddenly thought she should like to go. He was introduced, and had the honour of dancing with the Lady Maud, the second daughter of the illustrious house. There was to be a cotillon. Everybody was talking about the Moldavian minuet that had been got up the night before at the house of the Duchess y Pommeros y Grenos y Giesleroso. No one could remember it. Her Grace of Ambleside was most anxious to see the figure reproduced; she had been told that there had been a Tarantella in it: Maud could do the

Tarantella—no one could do a Tarantella like Maud; she must see it; at all events try. Fortunately Horry had been at the Spanish Embassy. He explained the much desired figure, and added a few suggestions of his own; the Moldavian minuet was got up; Maud danced

the Tarantella. The Duchess was delighted. She thought Mr. Fortescue the most charming young man she had ever seen. Horry was asked to Kendal House.

It is said that every man has his opportunity once in a lifetime, which, if made the most of, leads on to fortune. The friendship of the Duchess of Ambleside was the opportunity of Horry Fortescue, and he cleverly availed himself of it. He suggested the blue and silver which was to furnish her Grace's boudoir; he designed, thanks to an artistic friend in the office, a series of *menu* cards of the most novel and elaborate description for her table; he bought her a gray parrot which could talk like an Irish Obstructive; his services were invaluable at picnics, garden-parties, and at lawn-tennis; he recommended works of devotion to the eldest daughter, gave sporting 'tips' to the second, and supported the third, who was in her teens, when she skated at Prince's. From 'such a charming young man' he soon developed into 'that dear Horry Fortescue.'

At the end of the season he was asked down to Ullsthwaite Castle for the shooting. He now schemed for his reward. There was a talk in the Department that Sefton Fitzgerald, the Duke's private secretary, was to become one of the Commissioners of Abbey Lands. Horry was most desirous of succeeding him. He begged the Duchess to use her good offices; and as her Grace had no poor cousin or favourite tutor to provide for, she readily consented to become his friend. The result was that at the end of a few weeks there appeared the following paragraph in the morning papers:

'We hear that Mr. Sefton Fitzgerald, of the Protocol Department, has been appointed a Commissioner of Abbey Lands. Mr. Fortescue, of the same department, will succeed Mr. Fitzgerald as private secretary to his Grace the Duke of Ambleside.'

Any one acquainted with official life is well aware that to be private secretary to a Cabinet Minister is one of the prizes in the Civil Service. Not only is the lucky recipient freed from the ordinary duties of his department, but he stands an excellent chance of being appointed to any of the staff posts in the service that may fall vacant—Commissionerships, Comptrollerships, Assistant-secretaryships, and the like. It is true that Horry has placed his foot on the first rung of the ladder of the State, but he has no intention of being content with his position. His calculating eye looks beyond, and he sees no obstacle to prevent him from attaining further successes. Already he enjoys the reputation of being a model private secretary. Search the Government service through, and there is not a man in it who knows how to receive a deputation with more urbanity or dismiss it with greater platitudes than

Horry Fortescue. To see him get rid of an Irishman who thinks he has a claim upon the Government is a marvel of tact, firmness, and diplomacy. At a glance he can distinguish the men whom he should introduce to his Chief from those he is able to deal with himself. The letters he writes are so terse and yet so courteous; no one has a happier knack than he of refusing without offence or accepting without responsibility.

Seated in his spacious room overlooking St. James's Park, with its rich mahogany furniture and imposing silver candlesticks, well dressed—never does he don that indescribable garment called an 'office-coat'—courteous, agreeable, dignified without *hauteur*, and easy without familiarity, he appears to the political visitor as a very fitting representative of the aristocratic traditions of the Protocol Department. The Duke is charmed with him, and vows that he never had a secretary who was so useful, and whose information can be so fully relied upon. As his Grace leans on the arm of Horry whilst walking down to the House of Lords on a fine afternoon, the friends of the young man who knew him at Harrow or Oxford—friends briefless in their chambers or poring over ledgers in their fathers' counting-houses, or who curse the 'service'—look at him enviously, and mutter to themselves, 'What luck some men have!'

It is true that Horry is a lucky man—the element of luck enters more into the affairs of life than philosophers suppose—but his post is no sinecure. There are few men in town more hard worked all the year round than

our private secretary. He is daily at the office at eleven; he has to read all the letters the Duke receives, from an important State paper to an application for an appointment from some one who stayed at the same hotel at Homburg with his Grace and gave him the address of a doctor; he receives visitors; he attends upon deputations; he has to hunt up references for the Duke's speeches, and furnish him with all departmental facts when the office is inquired into by the House; after the office is closed he has to attend upon his Chief at the House of Lords; when the Protocol Department is attacked by the Opposition he knows no rest either day or night, examining correspondence, wading through Blue-books, verifying references, and the like; whilst at the same time he has to put in an appearance at all great social entertainments, to accompany the Duke to public dinners, and out of the session to coach up his Grace in the current topics of the day, and find him material for speech-making. In short, Horry is amanuensis, aide-de-camp, public servant, literary man, official devil, man of fashion, and confidential correspondent all rolled into one.

He is occasionally to be seen within the walls of the Caravanserai. I am an elderly gentleman and what Horace—the poet, not the private secretary—calls *justa chiragra*, or in other words, gout afflicts considerably my extremities. Consequently my temper is somewhat peevish and irritable; and as my dinner chiefly consists of a basin of mutton-broth and a bottle of Apollinaris water, I am aware that my company does not much add to the gaieties of the table. But it is always a pleasure for me to meet young Fortescue. He is so very different from many of the *jeunesse dorée* of the present day, who are often only so many walking advertisements of their tailor, hatter, perfumer, and jeweller. He does not part his hair in the middle, or wear white gaiters, or swagger in his walk, or tilt his hat on one side, or cover his white well-shaped fingers with massive rings. He comes of a good stock, and has none of the pretence and self-assertion of the would-be gentry.

Whenever he dines at the club I try to secure the table next him. Living, as he does, among the great, he knows everything that is going on, and he imparts such information as he feels inclined to give with none of the mystery and importance of your fifth-rate man of fashion, but simply and naturally. He tells me what young women are going to the altar, and what young men are going to the dogs; what beauties are going to Court, and what fast men are going through it; he knows the latest good stories in circulation; he explains to my untutored mind the mysterious paragraphs in the newspapers relating to meditated divorces, turf frauds, and card scandals; his conversation is always amusing and, when he chooses, often instructive. Like most men who work hard, he is something of a *gourmet*, and it does my impaired digestion good to see him discuss his dainty little dishes and moisten his throat with the best club vintages.

But, unfortunately for me, Horry is not a frequent visitor at the Caravanserai. He belongs to the Blenheim and the Coterie, and the fascinations of those two superior establishments interfere greatly with the modest charms of my club. His official duties and crowd of invitations are also formidable obstacles to the ordinary routine of club life. Horry is a young man who 'will arrive' as the French say; and he knows perfectly well that to selfishly dine at the club, and afterwards to play whist till three in the morning, is not the course for him to adopt. He looks upon society as a woman does, not as a form of distraction, but as *a profession*. Cautious, calculating, self-seeking, good-tempered, good-looking, amusing, he takes stock of his advantages, and lays them out at the best interest he can command. He knows the fortunes of all the widows of his acquaintance, and can be frequently seen bending over the bulky volumes at the Probate Office—of course always for a friend. Perfectly aware that he is a 'detrimental,' and not an 'eligible,' he never attempts to enlist the affections of the few heiresses that cross his path, and consequently is highly thought of by prudent mothers. But a charming young widow! one who has been united to a wealthy elderly man, who has twined her simple guileless heart around his sexagenarian sympathies like ivy round a ruin, who has inherited all his fortune, and who has accordingly been cordially hated by all her husband's relations! I can fancy

young Fortescue's graceful figure, his winning manners, his deep-blue eyes, and silky beard, not entering the lists in vain in such a quarter. Horry's future is certain. He will marry money, he will enter the House of Commons, he will make a name for himself, and the time will assuredly come when, holding some good subordinate post—as Under-Secretary, or Junior Lord, or Vice-President—he will himself command the services of—a Private Secretary.

THE GUARDSMAN.

THE GUARDSMAN.

We can hardly imagine any one in this enlightened nineteenth century labouring under a state of social ignorance so profound as to be unacquainted with that great ornament to himself and to society—the Guardsman of the period. It may not have fallen to the lot of all to have shaken him personally by the hand, to have listened awe-struck to his lisping accents, to have been taken down by him to dinner, or, if we belong to the sterner sex, to have been taken up by him sharply for some misstatement we have made respecting the turf, the opera, or society generally. As regards the flesh we may, it is true, be strangers to each other; but O, thanks to the ever-flowing pen of the novelist, are we not intimately acquainted with his movements, his deeds, his conversations, his habits, his tastes, and all that belongs to him? Is not the name of the Guardsman synonymous with the most voluptuous luxury, the most perfect fashion, the most graceful indolence, the most brilliant wit, the noblest birth, the most charming combination of effeminacy and daring prowess; in short, with everything that woman admires and man envies? If you reply to this in the negative, all we can answer is, that you are no believer in modern novels.

It is my custom of an afternoon to enter the palatial halls of the Caravanserai, and to salt my buttered toast and drink my ante-prandial cup of tea whilst poring over the evening editions of the newspapers. I must confess to being partial to that social but somewhat indigestible institution, five-o'clock tea, and dawdle over the mild refection with all the love and languor of those who sipped bohea in the days of good Queen Anne. As a rule, scarcely am I seated in my roomy armchair, with the *Pall Mall Gazette*, the *Globe*, and the *Evening Standard* clutched in my selfish grasp, than Dolly Clavering, unless his arduous military duties interfere with his movements, comes in and sits down beside me. He, too, is fond of the exhilarating Chinese herb, and his tastes are considerably encouraged in that direction by a bevy of as fair sisters as ever donned tea-gowns. Dolly and I are excellent friends—'pals' is the expression he uses; and he is good enough to say that 'he has a regard, don't you know, for the old sportsman,' alluding to myself; though why I am a 'sportsman,' unless that in Dolly's phraseology everybody is a *sportsman*, is beyond me. Some of Dolly's friends call me an 'old fogey;' and if I am not to be designated by my rightful name, of the two I prefer to be termed an 'old sportsman.' There is a savour of manliness in the one which is not objectionable, but of womanliness in the other which is hardly flattering.

Dolly is a mere lad of one-and-twenty; and his bright, fresh, youthful face, with its nascent whiskers and moustache, the latter fondly caressed, the Clavering rather beaky nose, and his sisters' eyes, are as pleasant for a tired London man to look upon as are the snows of the Alps after the sands of the desert. A great buck is Dolly. His frock-coat fits his tall slender figure without a wrinkle; his trousers never break out into ugly folds at the knees; his boots are lacquered like polished ebony; his hat is new without being glossy; and there is a swagger, partly from diffidence, partly from hauteur, in his gait and greeting, which is seldom disagreeable in a very young man. Careful as is Dolly with respect to his attire, you could never mistake him for a dressy stockbroker or City swell; everything about him is quiet, sober, and unpretentious. Apart from liking young Clavering, and knowing something of his people, Dolly is regarded by me with a peculiar and special interest. He is a Guardsman, and has the honour to hold a commission in that favourite regiment the Bombardiers. Again let me say that Dolly is in the Guards.

I repeat the statement, for it appears to me that some curious delusions exist in the public mind as to the Guardsman of the period. He is the prize favourite of the novelists, and it must be confessed that *messieurs les romanciers* make him out to be a most wonderful personage. Only last night I read *Bearskin and Boudoir* by that favourite author of military fiction the fashionable Fitz-Jenkins. All the heroes of Fitz-Jenkins' works are soldiers, and it is needless for me to add, when a man boasts of an aristocratic prefix to a plebeian cognomen, that all his soldiers are Guardsmen, officers either in the Household Cavalry or in the Foot Guards. When I read of the doughty deeds of Dormer de Bohun Cholmondeley Beaumanoir (Fitz-Jenkins likes a good name for his hero), and think of Dolly, who is rather shy in ladies' society, and who prefers to go through a gate than over one when out with the hounds, the contrast is amusing.

Of course you know this Beaumanoir? What reader of fiction (and I own to being a most omnivorous novel-reader myself) is not acquainted with him? Are we not all familiar with his haughty commanding figure, his perfect features, those dark terrible eyes always being lit up with desire or revenge, the heavy moustache falling over the stern cruel mouth, the exquisitely modelled hands white as a beauty's, the arched instep, and the Arabian feet? And then the views of this splendid creature upon modern society! How fierce is the cynicism underlying all his opinions and judgments! When I listen to Fitz-Jenkins' heroes inveighing against the falsity of woman, and dealing out mordant strokes against the shams and hypocrisies of life in the club smoking-room, or in the *tabagie* of one of those ancient country mansions for which the pen of our author is noted, I compare him with Dolly, who can be seen any

Sunday morning during the season with his mother and sisters in the family pew at St. Peter's, Eaton-square, who is passionately fond of dancing, who is devoted to amateur theatricals, who loses what he is pleased to call his heart about half a dozen times a week, and who colours furiously when a woman snubs him (which is not often, for he is too shy and too much of a gentleman to be forward); and the contrast is striking.

What an ordinary man is Dolly Clavering, and what a brilliant creature is our Beaumanoir! When Dolly goes to ball or dance he is quite in a flutter of excitement if a reigning beauty will allow him to write his name on her card, or if some high dame of fashion asks for his escort to Hurlingham or the Orleans Club. Whereas Beaumanoir creates such havoc amid the duchesses and countesses, scattered liberally throughout Fitz-Jenkins' volumes, as to exhibit a most lamentable state of things in the English peerage. Haughty ladies, whose blood is so blue that it is surprising it condescends to flow at all, sigh for him; the greatest heiresses languish after his smiles; disappointment, rejection, refusal, are words never to be met with in his social dictionary. Dolly is not a bad man across country when his blood is up; but, as I have said, he regards jumping, unless when necessary, as a work of supererogation; he is a fair shot, and can knock over his pigeons at Hurlingham or the Gun Club as well as the generality of his fellows; nor is his performance despicable in the stubble and turnip fields, or in the coverts of the paternal woods. But Beaumanoir! He rides horses that none but he can ride; he never hunts but he is glued to the hounds from find to finish; whilst the gates, fences, brooks, doubles, and every mortal thing he takes with such consummate ease, always make the whole field tremble with fear. He eschews—dauntless and magnificent creature that he is!—ordinary sport—partridges, pheasants, grouse, and the like—and is only keen after big game. The tigers he shoots on foot; the wild buffaloes his unerring aim brings down; the lions, leopards, pumas, the whole Zoological Gardens, in fact, that fall to his wonderful breech-loader, are they not written in the pages of the veracious Fitz-Jenkins?

Unless when Dolly is on guard or engaged by society, he dines modestly at his club for some four or five shillings; then, while digestion is pleasantly waiting upon appetite, he pays a visit to the smoking-room and falls asleep over a novel; perhaps, when slumber has refreshed him, he goes up-stairs and takes a hand at whist, rigidly eschewing all bets, till it is time for him to go to his bachelor lodgings in Jermyn-street and turn into bed. We know how Beaumanoir, on the contrary, passes *his* time. What princely dinners he orders! what an educated *gourmet* he is! How deep are his potations, without ever affecting the clearness of his brain, the steadiness of his hand, or the basilisk coldness of his extraordinary eyes! How he gambles at *écarté*, napoleon, poker, baccarat, winning or losing thousands without ruffling the composure of that sphinx-like face or disturbing the serenity of that marble brow! How he has to hear from charming female lips of the misery his coldness, his indifference, or his neglect has caused in their too susceptible hearts! When I read of Beaumanoir—of his prowess, his Rochefoucauld maxims, his pampered tastes, his gorgeous attire, his innumerable conquests, and his Munchausen sporting adventures—it is a source of congratulation to me that I have never had the pleasure of seeing him amongst his comrades in the Household troops; for with all due deference to Fitz-Jenkins, it seems to me that Beaumanoir is a hard vicious brute, and far more like a flash groom who has been educated in the music-halls of the period than 'an officer and a gentleman.' If certain of our novelists hold the mirror up to Nature, well may society talk about the degeneracy of the British army. For my part, I do not believe in the accuracy of these descriptions—of what use is imagination unless you draw upon it?—and in refutation of such views and theories let me sketch the, I fear, somewhat commonplace career of Dolly Clavering.

The eldest son of an old Wiltshire squire and heir to some six thousand a year, Dolly, after a brief education at Eton, where he distinguished himself as one of the smartest 'fields' in the eleven, was gazetted to the Bombardiers. In these days of equality and open competition many of the privileges of the Guards have been docked; still a commission in one of its regiments will always be an object of envy to most young men. Living in London, except when quartered at Windsor or Shorncliffe, the Guardsman has every advantage that town life offers, and can enjoy to the full all the charms and fascinations of good society. Unlike his less fortunate brother in the Line, he knows nothing of dull provincial cities, with their barrack monotonies, garrison hacks, fifth-rate theatres, and indifferent amusements. He is exempt from foreign service; but in the hour of danger, and when the conflict is deepening around him, it is his special privilege to be in the front of battle. The uniform he wears is in my opinion the most becoming in the service. There are ladies who so admire the gauntlets, helmets, and cuirasses of the Life Guards and the Blues, and the gorgeous blue-and-gold of the Horse Artillery, that they vow no dress in the British Army equals them. But with all due deference to the opinion of the fair sex —and in matters of costume their judgment is not to be decried—when Dolly is adorned in his bearskin and well-fitting 'regimentals,' to use a word always employed by the ladies when describing the British officer in his war paint, no soldier, it seems to me, can wear a more

becoming uniform, or one which more unites grace with quiet splendour.

If we are to credit our novelists, the young Guardsman is always the handsomest of his sex, enjoys a most lavish allowance, dwells in sumptuous chambers in St.

James's-street, runs through a couple of fortunes before he has been five years on the town, disappoints his tradesmen, and then retires to some West India regiment or takes service under a half-savage potentate till the friendly heiress, who seems ever to be hovering over the colours of 'the Household,' takes pity upon him, and makes him once more a man and a millionaire. Dolly is certainly very good-looking, but for that advantage, it seems to me, he is more indebted to his father and mother than to the Guards. The old Squire gives his son a decent allowance, which enables him to pay his wine-merchant and his tailor, to keep a horse which he both rides and drives, and to have comfortable rooms on the second floor of a house in Jermyn-street—excepting to the adjutant no quarters are given to officers in the Guards in London. The paternal mansion is in Lowndes Street, but Dolly thinks it incumbent upon himself to live in apartments near his two clubs. He is known as a good son and a kind brother, and his people have little cause to complain of his desertion. Whenever he wants a dinner he has only to let his mother know that he will make one of the family party at eight o'clock for the cook to show all her cunning and the Squire to have up some of that 'Mouton' claret which has moistened the throats of the Claverings for well-nigh a generation. Having four charming sisters we need hardly say that Dolly finds no difficulty in obtaining the company of one or two men in his regiment on these occasions.

I have said that my young friend's allowance is good, but it is not exorbitant. Dolly has, however, one pull over his brother linesman—he is saved from many of the expenses which ordinarily attend an officer's life. Except when at Windsor or Shorncliffe he has no mess-bills to pay, nor is he called upon for incessant contributions; hence his income goes farther than it otherwise might. If Dolly draws five hundred a year from the kindly old man he calls 'the governor,' it is about as much as he does; and if a man does not gamble and is not the slave of any vicious tastes, five hundred a year when *spent rigidly upon oneself* will cover a fair expenditure. At all events Dolly does not live uncomfortably, he never seems to lack funds to dine his friends at the Caravanserai, to run over to Paris, to put in an appearance on first nights at the theatres, or to indulge in the various other forms of social distraction which require ready money. Nor should he; for I, *moi qui parle*, had a relative—the watch he picked up on the field of Waterloo after the engagement ticks before me as I write—who managed to live in the Guards on an allowance of three hundred a year, until he succeeded to his modest property; but, as Dolly reminds me, that was many years ago, and money went further then than it does now in these days of high wages, continual strikes, and increased expenditure. From what one hears, I fancy that the old Squire assists Dolly in the settlement of his accounts with his tailor and livery-stable keeper.

In reading novels one is always struck with the idleness of the Guardsman: he is making his hands white; he is adorning his outward man; he is flirting, lounging, eating, dancing, riding, driving, shooting, yachting, hunting, but never working. Far be it from me to say that Dolly's is an industrious or arduous life, yet it is not one that is 'all beer and skittles.' What with attending commanding officer's parade or adjutant's parade, and going on guard as a rule about every second day, he is not the complete idler and 'chalk soldier' many suppose. When on duty at St. James's or Buckingham Palace, or at the Tilt-yard, a grateful nation entertains him at St. James's Palace at a dinner, which costs the country some three thousand a year. At this dinner there are the three officers on guard at St. James's Palace (colonel, captain, and lieutenant), the two officers on guard at Buckingham Palace and the Tilt-yard, the three officers of the Life Guards—if they like to put in an appearance—and the guests of the evening; the colonel of guard inviting, unless he give a place to one of the juniors; if the Life Guards do not come their seats can be filled up. When it is the lot of the young Guardsman to march his men down to Threadneedle-street for the protection of that treasury of the nation, the Bank of England, the directors of that distinguished company furnish him with a neat little dinner, and even extend their hospitality to a couple of his friends when required; the Bank granting one bottle of port, sherry, or claret to each friend, and one bottle to the officer on guard. Occasionally Dolly asks me to be his guest, and, indolent youngster that he is, instead of marching his men along the Strand, Fleet-street, and Cheapside, he limits his pedestrianism to walking the soldiers to St. James's Park Station, and conveying them to their destination by the stifling but lazy process of travelling by the underground railway, the fares of course being defrayed out of Dolly's pocket. No wonder that the men have no objection to Mr. Clavering being on Bank guard!

When I dine in Threadneedle-street with Dolly, and look at my cheery host—the smart tunic discarded for the easy shooting-coat—I cannot but think how many young men have sat in that comfortable Bank parlour, and have drawn the curtain to sleep in that adjoining bedroom, with life and hope before them, and how various have been their careers! There was Jones, happiest and most amusing of private actors; he was shot down on that pitiless hillside of the Alma. There was Brown, who, after a brief career, and a decided refusal from his father to pay his bills, became bankrupt,

and is now a partner in a respectable wine-merchant's office in the east of England. There was Smith, the dullest soldier who ever cried out 'form fours' or 'shoulder arms,' but who is now a great military authority, and one of the shining lights in the House of Commons.

There was Robbynson, who, after that grievous love disappointment of his, exchanged arms for diplomacy, and is now Secretary of Legation somewhere across the Atlantic, and married, so they tell me, to a Creole—he who so raved about fair women! There was Snooks, a featherweight and the buck of his regiment, who is now sixteen stone, dresses like a farmer, and is great at agricultural dinners, ploughing matches, and in breeding stock. What a funny world it is! Those we thought fools are now the wise of the earth, the failures are brilliant successes, the poor have become rich, and those from whom we expected such great things have turned out the most commonplace of mediocrities. True it is that nothing is certain but the unforeseen, and that he is a sage man who can predict the future of his friends.

Still, in spite of this remark, I will take upon myself to cast the future of my friend, young Clavering. Unless the old Squire shall have been summoned by *pallida mors* to take his place in the vault of his ancestors beneath the aisle of the parish church at Trevennis, Dolly will remain in the Bombadiers, in all probability, till he obtains his company. For the next few years he will enjoy to the full, in all sobriety, I hope, the pleasures of the town. With all the buoyancy of youth he will let the future take care of itself, and bask in the sunshine of that present which seems eternal at one-and-twenty.

> 'Quid sit futurum cras, fuge quærere; et
> Quem sors dierum cunque dabit, lucro
> Appone; nec dulces amores
> Sperne puer; neque tu choreas,
> Donec virenti canities abest
> Morosa.'

The health of Dolly is excellent, and consequently he looks upon life through the rosiest of glasses. When he has money in his pocket he feels that the world is at his feet. He is easily amused; he believes in the sincerity of man's friendship; and in his opinion there are very few young women who are really ugly. We know that even under the humblest auspices life is enjoyable at that golden age of twenty. *Dans un grenier on est bien à vingt ans;* how much more then must it be enchanting when youth is to be passed amid all the *agréments* of existence that men generally care for? The typical Guardsman, it is true, is an awful cynic; but then think of those 'deep draughts' he is always taking, the dinners he eats daily, the love-making he has to go through, and ask yourself whether all that liquor, gormandising, and sensuality is not enough to upset the liver of even a transpontine hero—for after all cynicism is often only another word for spleen. And pray, why should a Guardsman be a cynic, and his comments always cruel, and his heart always savage? Is it a matter of such extreme dissatisfaction to be tolerably well born, to be the heir of a fair fortune, to be the *bien venu*, if you behave yourself, in the best London society, and a welcome guest in country house after country house? And why should he be biting and savage in his sarcasms? Why not make him, for a change, instead of a being 'sensual, earthly, devilish,' a frank, genial, kindly type of Young England, as in nine cases out of ten he is? Why let his love be always adultery, his wit always satanic, his courage always brutality, and his religion always unbelief? Has it ever struck the novelist that to be a Guardsman is not necessarily to be above all the ordinary feelings common to inferior mortals? Is he aware that the Guards were among the first to organise after the Crimean war a society the object of which was to relieve the distress in the squalid districts of London—in the fever-stricken haunts of Shoreditch, Bethnal-green, Whitechapel, and Westminster—and to relieve that distress *not* by deputy? 'Would he be surprised to hear' that gay young Guardsmen visited these haunts themselves, and distributed with their own 'snow-white hands' tickets for such plebeian articles of necessity as bread, meat, and coal? Yet such was the case, for the writer of these pages had the pleasure of assisting them in their labours.

Perhaps, by his sixth or seventh season, Dolly will begin to find that there is, after all, a certain amount of monotony in the distractions of society; that dinners and dances are a bore; that the gossip of the club is

dull; and that it is possible to have too much of polo, pigeon-shooting, cricket, lawn-tennis, and incessant excitement. His watchful mother and affectionate sisters will now make the most of this *ennui*; they will pass in review all the nice eligible girls they know of; a selection will be made; they will be trotted out for Dolly's inspection; the object of his preference will be made to frequently cross his path in town; she will be asked down to Trevennis in the autumn; a fond companionship will be struck up between her and Dolly's sisters; and one fine morning Adolphus Frederick Clavering, captain and lieutenant-colonel in the Bombardier Guards, will find himself standing at the altar-rails, ready to be offered as a victim to matrimony. As a married man and heir to a goodish property he will abandon soldiering, and betake himself to civil pursuits. By this time it is not improbable that the old Squire will be feeing Charon to ferry him over the Styx, and Dolly will succeed to the paternal fortune and honours. He will not be lavish or ostentatious, for his fortune will not permit of extravagance; yet his house will be by no means closed to the country around, or to his various London friends. He will be put into the commission of the peace, and when he goes to Court he will wear the scarlet uniform of a deputy-lieutenant. He will hunt a good deal, till he gets fat and his nervous system begins to break down. He will be always fond of shooting, for sight generally lasts longer than nerves. He will be a good landlord, and interest himself moderately in agricultural matters. If he has a few hundreds to throw away, and wants occupation, he may amuse himself by farming the home-farm on his own account. His wife and children will look after the poor. He will be on good terms with his vicar, and make a point of putting in an appearance in the square curtained pew of the parish church every Sunday morning. He will come up to town for three months in the year, and as he gets older abuse the change from the country to London. In short, he will be a model country gentleman, and he will be none the less popular in his county, and none the worse husband and father, because he is a man of the world, and in his youth was a Guardsman.

PATRIOTISM.

PATRIOTISM.

We are told that imitation is the sincerest flattery; and if this be the case, the Frenchman ought by no means to feel his self-love wounded at the homage his country nowadays meets with at our hands. It was once the distinctive characteristic of England that she was not like other continental nations. Her manners, her tastes, her architecture, the habits of her men, the dresses of her women, were all very different from the customs that reigned abroad. It might be difficult at first sight to distinguish between a Frenchman and an Italian, a Spaniard and a Portuguese, a Russian and a German; but an Englishman carried unmistakably his nationality in his face, his walk, and the manner in which he took off his hat. As we were cut off from other countries by our insulated position, so were our inhabitants cut off from other people by their insulated tastes and characteristics. We piqued ourselves upon being cleaner in our habits, more refined in our sanitary arrangements, manlier in our tastes and sports, and at heart more moral and religious in our approval and condemnation of things. We thought that in the 'foreigner' there was little calculated to excite our envy or admiration, and by the word 'foreigner' we generally signified the Frenchman. France was our hereditary foe; she was always threatening our shores; she was the disturber of the peace of Europe; her wit had severely satirised the institutions of our country, and between the two nations little love was lost. To the Frenchman we were *la perfide Albion*, a nation of shopkeepers, a people with no taste for the fine arts, puritanical in our creed, and good only to breed horses and brew beer. To the 'honest John Bull type' of Englishman the son of Gaul had the manners of a dancing-master, the morals of a courtesan, the dress and appearance of a billiard-marker—a man filthy in his personal habits, effeminate in his tastes, and one whose favourite food was frogs and whose favourite drink was sugar-and-water.

However, thanks to steam and electricity, our prejudices have undergone considerable modification, and, instead of despising the Frenchman, we now run to the other extreme, and import many of his customs with most of his wines to our shores. Slowly but surely our English institutions are becoming Frenchified. Our fashions are copied from those in Paris; our cooks serve up French dishes; the most modest restaurant thinks it incumbent upon itself to translate its thoroughly English bill of fare into the language of France; every hotel that comes into existence offers us that most dull and dreary of all festivities, an English *table d'hôte;* thin sour wines, maliciously labelled clarets and burgundies, have ousted old October ale and old dry port from the cellar; the startling views of domesticity so dear to the French novelist and playwriter have been introduced into our fiction and upon our stage. In spite of the treacheries of our climate, the familiar *café* of the boulevards has been transported into certain of our streets; the games at cards that are now most popular with our youth are those that are freely played in the *cercles* of Paris; whilst the one great stronghold of the country, the English day of rest, is gradually being transformed by the social hospitalities of the fashionable and the efforts of the philanthropist into the Sunday of the Continent.

I am not for a moment saying that these changes are an improvement or the reverse. I simply state a fact patent to all—that our institutions are becoming Frenchified. And *la belle France* has paid us a similar compliment. As we have adopted, or flatter ourselves that we have adopted, her toilettes, her vintages, her cookery, her gaiety, her morality, her games of chance, so she has introduced our Turf nomenclature into her language, our stallions into her stud, our jockeys into her stable, the strain of our hounds into her packs, pale ale into her drinks, the wares of Savile-row into her sartorial establishments, and built her carriages upon English lines. The result of this reciprocity has been to create in both nations a class of men which, whilst maligning the habits and institutions of its own country, blindly worships all that belongs to its neighbour. We have at Paris the Frenchman who so warmly admires our club-life in Pall Mall, the beauty of our women, the breed of our horses, the freedom of our government, the manliness of our field sports, the cleanliness of our tastes, that, surveying his own fair land from Picardy to Gascony, and from Brittany to Franche Comté, he finds it stale, flat, and unprofitable, and that out of England there is nothing worthy of envy or acceptance. At London we have the man who is always instituting comparisons between our capital and Paris, very much to the disadvantage of the former, who curses our climate, our architecture, our ill-dressed women, our wretched cookery, our servility to the powers that be, our vulgarity, our mock-modesty, our inappreciation of all true art; our love of beer, which makes us gross; our love of field sports, which makes us brutal—in short, everything that belongs to us and our country.

Prominent among this band of Anglophobists is Luttrell Chichester, who, on the few occasions that he visits 'that damned city of yours,' as he is pleased to call the London of his fathers, makes his home at the Caravanserai. A younger son, he was passing his time as one of the second secretaries of her Majesty's embassy at Vienna, copying despatches, and making a *précis* of reports touching the growth and development of Austrian commerce, when, by the whim of a cousin, he became the heir to a fair property situated in the not very beautiful district of East Lincolnshire. To quit diplomacy, to let his newly acquired estate, and to settle in Paris were, as the novelists say, the work of a moment. To be in Paris, and of Paris, had always been the ambition of Chichester. When in the diplomatic service he had exerted all his interest to be attached to our embassy at that bright capital; but the Fates and the Foreign Office had declined to listen to his wishes. He had been sent to Stuttgardt, then to Dresden, then— this exchange was delightful—to Ispahan, and then to Vienna; but never once had he had occasion to don his diplomatic uniform at a ball or *levée* at the Tuileries. Therefore as soon as he was a free man, and his bankers' book permitted him to enjoy without stint all the fascinations of life, he made Paris his home.

He was precisely the man to appreciate the pursuits and pleasures of this the gayest of cities—the gayest because it is the capital not only of France, but of Europe. He was a Catholic, but his religion sat lightly upon him, never pricking his conscience or interfering with his amusements, yet always ready to soothe him when bilious or disappointed; it was not a curb or a fetter, but an anodyne. He was well-read in the sense that a Frenchman is well-read; he was familiar with the light literature of most countries; he knew most of the great tragedies and comedies that had been written; he was well up in modern history; he had a good practical acquaintance with geography and political economy; he had a keen appreciation of wit and humour; and he knew enough Latin to read the Odes of Horace. He was an epicure; he was fond of amusement; he was addicted very far from wisely to the society of the fair sex; and he could give and swallow any amount of flattery. Between him and the typical Englishman there was little in common. In the tastes and habits of Luttrell Chichester there was a touch of effeminacy. He was fond of ostentation, and was perfectly free from our national *mauvaise honte*. He cared far more to flirt in a boudoir than to ride across country. Spending a great deal of time over his personal appearance, and setting up for a lady-killer of the most seductive description, he was never so happy as when surrounded by women, complimenting them, escorting them, and carrying out their behests. To such a man—whose fortune permitted him to gamble at his *cercle*, whose birth and religion did

not exclude him from the exclusive assemblies of
the Faubourg St. Germain, who was well introduced
into the amusing and cosmopolitan society of the capital
—Paris possessed attractions such as no other city could
offer. After a couple of winters, Chichester resolved to
look upon France as his home, and to substitute Paris
for London.

For all practical purposes, he is now as complete a
Frenchman as if he had not been born this side of the
Channel. He rents a flat near the Champs Elysées,
and a small château near Fontainebleau. He is a member of the Bébé Club. He swears fealty to the white flag,
and is the most loyal of those who regard Henri Cinq as
their king. In his dress, and in the appointments of his
chambers and of his country seat, he slavishly imitates
the fashions of the land of his adoption. He eschews
the society of the English at Paris. He trims his hair,
shaves his cheeks, and curls his moustache like a Frenchman. He takes his two meals a day like a Frenchman.
He interests himself alone in French politics, and works
himself into a passion when the German victories, the
annexation of Alsace and Lorraine, and the movements
of M. Gambetta are mentioned. When he has occasion
to speak English he shrugs his shoulders and gesticulates like the true Gaul; and when he talks to an
Englishman of England, he alludes to her as 'your

country.' He has obtained a title from the Pope, and has blossomed forth into the Chevalier Chichestère. Ashamed of our island and avoiding her people, he has so identified himself with French interests and French manners, that when he is called *un Anglais* he feels himself insulted. It must be admitted, however, that his impersonation of the Frenchman is a great histrionic success; he both speaks the language and looks the character to perfection.

When Chichester enters the Caravanserai during one of his short visits to London, the waiters always look upon him as one of our distinguished foreign members, and treat him accordingly. He wears a peculiar hat, very shiny, very narrow brimmed, and very arched; he looks at life out of the lenses of a *pince-nez;* a heavy moustache falls over his mouth, whilst a little *mouche* (it was an imperial, you know, in the days of the Empire; now, under the Republic, it is a *mouche*—for MacMahon wears one—how suggestive this is of man's fidelity!) nestles in the curve above the chin; his cheeks are blue and shaven like those of a priest; very loose all-round collars, with a spotted tie made into a bow, with wide pendulous ends, encircle his neck; his cutaway coat and waistcoat have that peculiar tightness and inelegance of the Parisian tailor; the trousers, often wonderful in pattern (lavender and the Mackenzie tartan for choice), fit tight to the leg, and fall over a snow-white pair of gaiters; whilst the boots are short and very broad at the toes. No wonder that men accustomed to the works

of art of Poole, Lock, and Thomas regard Chichester as a foreigner. As he walks up our morning-room he adopts a little mincing gait; when he talks to you or sits down to read the newspaper he puts himself into attitudes; and when he has occasion to find fault, he pouts and waves his hands like a girl. The wags at the Caravanserai have christened him Henrietta.

He is a source of great amusement to many of the members. In his diatribes against England there is no affectation of animosity; he really and unfeignedly detests the country, its climate, institutions, and inhabitants. When he takes his walks abroad he returns to the club sick at heart and sincerely disgusted. He has seen toilettes that have made his fastidious nerves shudder as if he had listened to a false note in music; the dust has gone into his eyes and down his throat; the watering-carts have flooded the land where he wants to cross the road. '*We* lay the dust,' he says, with his girlish pout; 'you make mud.' The hot streets have been unshaded by trees, whilst no cool enticing *café* has been there to offer him repose and refreshment; he has been shaken about in a dirty and miserably-hung cab; he has been bored by the dead-level of dulness and monotony that is everywhere visible. 'No wonder,' he says, as he takes up the *Figaro*, 'that you boast of your home life in this damned country of yours, for nobody who could help it would ever go out of doors.' He dines out at the houses of his sisters, and at the houses of friends he feels bound once a year to meet, and he mourns over the bad wines he has to drink, the indigestible dishes that he has to eat, the bad ventilation of the rooms, the solemnity of the men, and the want of tact of the women. 'To thoroughly appreciate Bignon's,' he sneers, 'you must have dined in England. To know what dress is without taste, what conversation is without sparkle, what hospitality is without grace, you must enter London society.'

We take him to the theatres; we show him Mr. and Mrs. Bancroft, we show him Mr. and Mrs. Kendal, we show him Mr. Hare, we show him Mr. Irving; we ask him to weep over our tragedies, to laugh over our comedies, and to split his sides over our burlesques; but his face never relaxes its rigid expression of utter boredom. '*Mon Dieu*, and those are your actors and actresses!' he yawns, as he quits the theatre. 'What a pity it is you do things by halves! You get your plays from Paris; why not get your actors?' If he wishes to dine away from the club, where, he plaintively asks, can he go? At his beloved Paris he has the Café Anglais (I have dined with him there in No. 16—or rather sat down to dinner, for dyspepsia does not permit me to indulge—and can speak of him most favourably as a host), the Maison Dorée, Bignon's, and several other haunts well known to the French *gourmet*. 'Whilst here,' he cries, 'your best restaurants, now that Francatelli is dead, are a disgrace even to the Palais Royal.' It is impossible to please him; everything he sees, everything we do, everything we praise, is a mistake, and gives rise to the ridicule of Europe. Like ancient Rome and ancient Greece, like Venice and Spain, England has seen her best days, and is fast going to wreck and ruin. '*Sapristi!*' he says, with his girlish gesticulations, 'you are a droll people! In your newspapers and at your clubs you imagine yourselves a powerful nation, and that your voice is a potent one in the councils of Europe. Yet cross the Channel, and what notice do you find any of the Powers taking of the views and feelings of England? *Rien!* You are a shop, not a barrack, and what else can you expect? You look upon politics only through the medium of commercial interests, and then wonder at the decline of your national prestige. You encourage pusillanimity, and call it arbitration. You weaken strength, and call it reduction. You impair efficiency, and call it economy. You exchange a patriotic aristocracy for a mischievous middle class, and then wonder at misgovernment. You ridicule Protection, and then wonder at commercial panics and agricultural distress. You legalise trades-unions, and then marvel at the antagonism between labour and capital. You sanction the freedom of the press, and then are astonished at the spread of sedition. *Mon Dieu*, your country is going to the devil, and it won't be much of a catch when he gets it!' Luttrell Chichester, I fear, will.

He is particularly wrath with the conduct of the

English who visit his fondly cherished city. He objects to the style of dress they adopt, to their open contempt for the manners of the country, to their arrogance, brutality, and utter want of *savoir-faire*.

'Why, if you were Germans,' he sneers, 'you could not behave worse! Why walk about the Boulevards as if you were going out cover-shooting? Why, when you dine together, talk at the top of your voice, and let all Paris know that you are English? Why refuse to be courteous to a man or woman simply because he or she happens to stand behind a counter? Why, when shut up at a railway station waiting for your luggage, or standing at a box-office waiting for a ticket for the theatre, or at a review, or on the racecourse, always insist in the loudest of tones upon the superiority of your own institutions, and make yourselves thoroughly objectionable to all around you? At Paris you are simply hated, and if it were not for your money you would be treated with marked disrespect.'

'You are quite right to stand up for Paris,' replies a youngster, who has just entered upon his forensic career as judge's marshal; 'it is the jolliest place out! If I had my way I'd be like you, and live over there. Give me an invite at Easter, Chichester.'

'Paris the jolliest place out!' sardonically laughs Chichester. 'That is the way with you young fellows. Pray what do you know of Paris? You put up at an hotel where a Parisian never enters; you walk arm-in-arm along the Boulevards, and inspired by the romances of Paul de Kock and Xavier de Montépin, imagine that you are to enter into an intrigue with the first great lady you meet in your promenade; you drive to the Bois or up and down the Champs Elysées in a two francs and a half fly; you dine by yourselves, and drink too much at the Café Anglais or at Bignon's, and then, flushed and noisy, you sally forth to a theatre, where you don't understand the language, or to the Mabille or the Closerie des Lilas, where you *do* understand the language, and finish your day with a supper at Brébant's, in society which even the clerk of a *notaire* would consider compromising. And then you say there is no place like Paris, and flatter yourselves you know what life in Paris is! You bring no letters of introduction with you; you do not know a single lady of fashion to ask you to a dance or to dinner; you belong to none of the *cercles*; you are not acquainted with a single political or literary celebrity to show you any attention; and yet you return to London and say, "Awfully jolly place, Paris! Know every inch of it! Never was more amused in my life! You go and see *Niniche*."'

Chichester, however, is one of the few Englishmen who really is acquainted with Paris. He has been good enough to invite me to stay with him both at his chambers and at his charming little country seat. Under his auspices I am able to form some idea of what Parisian life is. He takes me into society, which I am not surprised to find is very different from that depicted by certain novelists and dramatic authors; at his hospitable breakfast-table one meets authors, actors, and the 'curled darlings' of the Bébé and the Jockey Club; he has introduced me at the greenroom of the Français;

he has obtained tickets for me to listen to debates at Versailles; and, thanks to him, I have sat amongst the crush on the admission of an Academician. He drives me to neighbouring races in his drag—driving like a Frenchman, with his arms sticking out from his

sides, and his body well forward; he puts my name down as an honorary member at a *cercle*, where I can play baccarat if it pleases me to the most unlimited extent; he tells me what to see, whom to know, and what to avoid. He is as different a companion in France as a London fog is from an Italian sky. Bright, cheery, amusing, full of anecdote and geniality, he has little in common with the discontented, dyspeptic, surly denizen of Pall Mall that he is when in England.

But to see him at his best you must stay with him at his château near Fontainebleau. There he is the complete French country gentleman, as on the Boulevards he is the complete *flâneur*. Dressed in a suit of yellow jean, with a large Leghorn straw hat on his head, he goes pottering about his trim gardens, with their succession of terraces, formal flower-beds, mimic fountains, and yews cut into all manner of fantastic shapes, whilst the shaved poodle trots by his side; or else he pays a visit to his little home farm, well stocked with Breton cows, Auvergne sheep, pigs from Westphalia, Spanish poultry, and white huge-flanked Norman horses. He is a kind landlord, and is on excellent terms with the curé of the village, to whom his donations *pour les pauvres* are very liberal. As becomes a Legitimist, and one on whom the pious regions of the Faubourg St. Germain smile kindly, in the country he is most respectable, and never misses attending high mass on Sundays or on the great festivals, acting as escort to some high dame engaged in collecting *une quête*. In Paris he does as he pleases, but in the country he has to set an example. When *la chasse* sets in, Chichester is in great force. In the coverts around he has plenty of birds, but it must be admitted that the pheasants and partridges have little to fear. Not only is Chichester a wretched shot, but the guests he fills his house with are little better. His shooting-parties are very delicious. The *petits crevés* and the *gommeux*,

who dawdle over breakfast, gorgeously attired in dark-green coats, black-velvet caps, jack-boots, and *couteaux de chasse* at their waistbelts, are in no hurry for the sport. They chat, smoke cigarettes, look at themselves in the glass, and then, when the morning is fast dissolving into the afternoon, make up their minds to face the cold air. Each one has his man behind him with a couple of guns; but the young Gauls are far more accustomed to the pavement of Paris than to the ridge and furrow of the fields, or the yielding leafy rides in the woods. They do not attempt to keep in line; they never think of preserving silence; they point the barrels of their breechloaders at each other with a charming contempt for the consequences of manslaughter; they blaze into a thick covert heedless of dogs, beaters, or a brother sportsman; and if they make a bag, which we should consider most moderate if it fell to one gun, they are in ecstasies. They want female society, music, or absinthe to wake them up and give them energy; and I am sure in their heart of hearts they curse the damp, the cold, and long for the evening and to bid for the bank at baccarat. It was the same when they went out hunting. Attired in a costume something between a circus-master and an Odd Fellow, they were only happy when riding to cover or when saying charming nothings to the fair amazons who turned up at the meet; but when the hounds were thrown in by the huntsman into a furze-brake, and when the music of their tongues plainly told that the fox had been found, then the Frenchmen looked uncomfortable. They fidgeted about, altered their stirrups, and, before they had made up their minds to jump a two-feet ditch, men, horses, and hounds were fields ahead, and our 'sportsmen' were hopelessly thrown out.

No, Chichester, most prejudiced of Anglophobists, in spite of all your teaching, give me old England! Johnny Crapaud may be very well in his way. I grant you he is very amusing and generally very lively; but he wants ballast, he promises more than he performs, his sincerity is not to be depended upon, he is not wholesome in many of his tastes, and he is too fond of 'a gallery' and of showing off to be really in earnest or really manly. John Bull, with all his faults, is the more sterling of the two, as he always was and always will be.

LETTERS.

LETTERS.

THE successful man of letters at the present day has little to complain of. Time was when he had to haunt the antechambers of the great, to badger the whole circle of his acquaintance for subscriptions, and to sell his political opinions to the first statesman who wanted them, ere he could eke out a livelihood sufficient to liberate him from the clutches of the sheriff's officer and from the dens of the Fleet. It was a red-letter day with him when he had received his ten guineas for a dedication to a peer who wished to pose as a patron of letters at a modest cost, or when his list of subscribers was full enough to justify him to go to press with his new volume, or when he was offered a collectorship in the Customs or the Revenue because his squibs and his satires had been useful to a Minister. In those 'dark ages' of literature the reading public was limited, and the author, unless favoured by the great or the State, soon found that his audience was too small or too indifferent to support him.

One little source of pride, however, remained to him; he might have to starve as Otway starved; he might have to find his bed, like Savage, on the garbage of the market-place; he might be ill-clad, dunned, and arrested; but he was an *author*—a man of education whose opinions were respectfully listened to, who received the homage

of the set in which he lived, and whose pen commanded for him a consideration that he would not otherwise have obtained. Authorship was then, not as now a profession, but a distinction. To have written a book, whether it succeeded or was damned, was in itself an accomplishment which raised the writer a full head and shoulders above the common herd. It qualified him for admission into society, it ushered him into the presence of the powerful, he was treated with deference by all, saving those who had pecuniary relations with him, and he was regarded as amongst the notables of the coffee-house that he frequented. If his book was talked about, and he was born under the star of a Minister who encouraged letters and the fine arts, he might find himself performing the duties of a sinecure commissionership, and drawing a handsome salary from the Treasury. He might hold the seals of a Secretary of State like Addison; he might be a Commissioner of Appeals like Locke; a Master of the Mint like Newton; a Commissioner of Stamps like Steele; or be attached to embassies as were Gay, Prior, and Stepney.

It was, however, all a question of luck. If a Minister like Walpole or the second Pitt stood at the helm of government, the author, the poet, and the satirist had a hard time of it. No snug post under the Crown then fell to his lot; he was attached to no embassies; his old age was cheered by no pensions; as he had made his bed so must he lie upon it. 'If you are such a damned fool,' said Sir Robert Walpole, with his characteristic delicacy of feeling, to a poor author, 'as to follow a trade that does not pay, you have only yourself to blame. If the State is to help all who have been unsuccessful in their calling, the Exchequer would be empty to-morrow, and I do not see why the country should assist one whose books publishers cannot sell, or whose plays managers cannot act, more than one who fails in any other form of business.' Had old Sam Johnson lived in the reign of Queen Anne, a high government appointment would have effectually relieved him from slaving for the publishers and from the drudgery of hack-work. On the other hand, had Congreve lived in the days of George II. or of George III. he would simply have remained a writer for the stage, and have been dependent upon his own exertions for his income. The pursuit of literature was in itself a miserable occupation; it might lead to advantages, but such advantages were unconnected with the calling of authorship pure and simple. Until the present century, with the exception of Pope and Dryden, it is doubtful whether any single author managed to subsist comfortably upon the profits that arose from the sale of his works. Sir Walter Scott was accustomed to say that the pursuit of literature was a bad staff, but a good stick; in the 'good old times,' however, the calling of a man of letters was neither a staff nor a stick, but the slenderest of reeds.

Happily a healthier state of things has been ushered in. Education has been busy with the masses, circulating-libraries have been established, cheap newspapers flood the land with their broadsides, and the consequence is that a vast reading public, eager after novelty and attractive information, has been called into existence. A man who hits the literary taste of the day is sure, not only of popularity, but of the substantial rewards of ready money. He need not pander to the cheap vanity of a patron; there is no necessity for him to go hat in hand begging for subscribers, nor has the penurious certainty of a small government appointment any attractions for him. His patron is the public, and as long as it reads his works, so long will publishers gladly pay him for his wares and the libraries order their hundreds of copies. Literature is now a profession, like law or medicine, and the successful author enjoys the same rank and receives the same homage as any other successful professional man. The mere fact of having written a book in these days, when everybody reads and almost everybody writes, is in itself no mark of distinction; should the work make a 'hit,' the author is treated by the world with the same consideration that it accords to the rest of the pedestrians who have distanced their fellows on the high-road to fame. He is a fortunate man, precisely as the barrister whose tables are covered with briefs is a fortunate man, or the doctor who is gaining a large practice, or the engineer who is full of contracts, or the merchant who freely prospers is a fortunate man. The days are past when an author is stared at by society because a publisher has given his manuscript to the world. We worship success of all kinds, and if our friend of the pen becomes talked about we follow in his train, yet not, as in the days of the Tudors and the Stuarts, because he is a writer, but because he is successful. Literature has no longer a pedestal to itself, but takes its place in the sculpture-gallery with the rest of the statuary, and is bought and criticised like the other figures that surround it, and vulgarly valued for what it will fetch. The divinity that once hedged round the author has departed, and in its stead is the tradesman with his scale of profits and losses, and who knows to an ounce what is the true worth of 'copy.' Empty homage has given way to solid bullion.

That the calling of a successful literary man is not to be despised is evidenced by the career of one of the pillars of the Caravanserai, familiarly called 'Jimmy.' Why he should be known as Jimmy, considering that, according to the wishes of his godfather and godmother, he was christened Hugh, and that the family name is Lister, it is beyond me to discover. One thing is, however, certain, that he is always called Jimmy, and to speak of him as Lister is to brand oneself as an ignoramus, an outsider, and utterly unworthy of membership of the Caravanserai. Quite a representative man is Jimmy. In the smoking-room his easy-chair is always the centre of attraction; for his stories are amusing, his conversation

witty, and he possesses precisely that information upon things in general and scandal in particular which is suited to the hour of one o'clock in the morning. He is the great authority in the club upon literature, the drama, and the fine arts. The gossip of the greenroom is at his fingers' ends; and he is not reticent upon the feuds of actors and the witcheries of actresses. He knows all the new works that are coming out, what novels are to be naughty or insipid, and explains all the mysterious allusions in the newspapers, and the classical quotations that may crop up in the course of talk or perusal. Having once painted a picture that was rejected, he developed into the art-critic of a leading journal, and his remarks, if biting, are amusing on the intrigues of the Royal Academy, the jealousies of artists, and on that burlesquing of Nature which English people call art.

Jimmy is a general favourite, for he has a great deal in his power, and is not unlavish in its disposal. The newspaper of which he is editor and part proprietor is always open to puff his friends who write books, paint pictures, or mould busts; he is always ready, unless in the full swing of the parliamentary season, to spare a paragraph for the achievements of the 'spring-captains' and the 'sportsmen' who are amongst the number of his acquaintance — for their Alpine ascents, their rowing-matches against time, their hunting of the big game in South America, or their racing, driving, yachting, and running deeds. His pen and kindly words are ever prompt to introduce a friend, or friend's friend, who is supposed to have literary or artistic talent, to the publishers, the picture-dealers, and the editors of magazines and reviews. From his journalistic position and his acquaintance with managers and actors he seldom lacks 'orders' for the theatre and the opera, and when these are in his possession he generously gives them to those in the club who he thinks will most appreciate the present —barristers whose briefs have not yet arrived, young government clerks whose seniors decline to make way for them, soldiers on half-pay, and the rest of the fraternity of social paupers. The well-to-do suppliants —and it is astonishing how many of the wealthy petition for orders—he dismisses with a caustic gibe at their meanness to the libraries and box-offices.

Whenever anything is to be done and wherever anything is to be seen there to be sure is Jimmy. If an ironclad is going to be launched, a new bridge to be opened, a grand field-day to be held at Aldershot, a naval review to take place at Spithead, a banquet to be given to a distinguished personage, Jimmy is certain to be presented with a card. And as for the tickets for race-meetings, 'first nights,' private views at exhibitions, concerts, City dinners, and for all the other forms of the external dissipation of London society that crowd his looking-glass and mantelpiece, their number is legion. No wonder, then, that a man who has so much in his gift, who is such excellent company, and who is the most perfect of hosts, should be much sought after and be deemed the most popular of good fellows. He has but one enemy, and that is his tailor, whom he will never permit to dress him in the fashion; Jimmy running to flesh prefers his habits loose, and declines to be buttoned up and puckered and encased in the manner sartorial art delights in.

It is not unusual with me to cross the Park of a morning, and call upon Jimmy at his chambers in Victoria-street whilst he is breakfasting at an hour when ordinary people are lunching. When I enter his rooms, furnished in the most approved mediæval style, and criticise their luxurious appointments—the easy-chairs, the valuable engravings, the rare books, the china, and curious glass that juts out from the wall on velvet brackets, the old brass and mirrors and oak cabinets—or watch their owner enjoying life to the full, surrounded by all that modest ambition can desire, the thought frequently crosses my mind, How different is the fate of Hugh Lister from that of many of his predecessors!

When I see Jimmy giving his little dinners at the club at a certain well-known round table, the waiters active and attentive, the chief butler himself superintending the serving of the dishes, the champagne iced to perfection, the claret warmed with the most consummate care—I think of the men, better read than he, and endowed with greater talents, who knew not where to turn for a meal or a couch, calling themselves lucky if they could dine at a tripe-shop or pay for the shelter of a garret. I think of the author of *Venice Preserved* choking himself over the food, from which he had been so long deprived, in the fierce greed of hunger; of the ill-starred Savage crouching for warmth before the dying ashes of a glass furnace; of the great Orientalist, the translator of the Koran, pursuing his studies amid the severest privations; of old Sam Johnson, hidden behind the screen in the publisher's dining-room, because his coat was too ragged to admit him to the table of his host; of Steele, Goldsmith, Smollett, Fielding, Crabbe, Chatterton, and the hundred and one other brothers of the pen, who knew often what actual want was, what misery was, what pain left to itself was, and what followed from the grasp of the sheriff's officer!

When I see Jimmy on his famous three-hundred-guinea cob, well up to eighteen stone, and whose head and crest and quarters are the admiration of the Row, or driving his pair of bays about the town or the suburbs, there rise before me visions of pale sad faces who have had to part with their manuscripts, their poems, their satires, their tragedies, their essays and novels, for a tenth or a twentieth of the sum our nineteenth-century scribe gives for one of his horses. Did not Milton sell his incomparable epic for the price of a new saddle? Can you buy a stanhope at a good maker's for the price at which Goldsmith sold his *Vicar of Wakefield?* Did not Dryden engage himself to write ten thousand verses for less than the price of an opera-box for the season? Was not *Evelina* parted with by Miss Burney at the price of a frock-coat? And pray what did the men of letters under the first three Georges make out of literature? But perhaps the saddest of all reflections is how fared it with the men, then as now, who could find no publisher to take their wares, whose tastes and peculiarities of character unfitted them for the ordinary occupations of life, who read and wrote in the hope of one day receiving their reward and having their niche in the Temple of Fame, only to find their end in the gaol, the hospital, or the terrible exit of the suicide? As I write there stands out against the background of the past the lean haggard form of one I knew, who busied himself with subjects that appealed to the few, who degenerated into a publisher's hack; then even that calling failed him, for others could be found to do the work cheaper; who was poor unto misery, yet neither his garb nor conversation revealed his sorrows, for the pride of manhood made him keep his poverty to himself, till anxiety and suffering bade him one fatal day brave the terrors of the unknown, and put an end to the life, whose burden was greater than he could bear, by his own hand. Poor soul! had one but known how severe was the measure the Fates had dealt out to him, he needed not have been fearful again of distress or privation; gladly subscriptions would have been raised for him: but he kept us all in ignorance of his affairs, and whilst we mourn his reserve, we cannot but respect the pride and pluck that dictated it. How many suffering hearts have thus passed to their rest, conscious of the genius working within them, their brains stored with the intellectual accumulations of ages, yet rudely ignored by the times in which their lot was cast, whilst the empty and the frivolous were the idols of the hour! To obtain success is not always to deserve it. Life is but a lottery, and it is quite as often that a prize is drawn by a fluke as by desert.

Not that by this digression I am inferring that Jimmy is not deserving of his prosperity. Far from it; no man works harder or is more worthy of the success that attends him: only there are others to the full as able as himself, and who work quite as assiduously, yet somehow their names are known to the few, and their wares have little market value. Let us see how Jimmy raised himself to the position of a favourite of Fortune. The son of an ex-cavalry officer, who was atoning for the dissipation of his youth and the loss of the paternal acres over hazard by strict economy at the little town of Dinan in Brittany, young Lister received his first education at the hands of the parish priest, a Jesuit well schooled in mathematics and who knew the

classics as his Breviary. Sharp, studious, and a keen observer of all that fell within his ken, the lad was a most promising pupil, and soon showed of what he was capable. He was sent to a grammar-school in Kent which had numerous exhibitions at Oxford; two of these young Lister gained, and passed himself through the University without costing his impecunious parent a single sou. Disappointed in obtaining a fellowship, he came to London and entered himself at the Bar. He had his name painted in the blackest of letters on the yellowest of backgrounds, he went circuit, he went sessions, he attended the courts at Westminster; but solicitors declined to honour him with their patronage. At last he put his wig in its tin box, hung up his gown, and betook himself to that great refuge of the unsuccessful forensic mind—journalism. He had succeeded to the family property of two hundred a year, and what with reviews, magazine articles, and occasional leaders, he managed to live in Dryden's Buildings, not uncomfortably, nay with splendour compared to many of the barristers who lodged on his staircase. Finding that works of imagination, if successful, were the most lucrative of all literary productions, he wrote a novel. It was rejected by the trade. Young authors, take heart from this, and be not cast down! The first novel of the popular Jimmy was refused; why, then, need you despair? What is the general fate of first efforts? What are Raphael's 'Dream' and Gibbon's *History of Switzerland* but miserable failures? Were not the first appearances of Kean, Kemble, and Mrs. Siddons cordially hissed? Were not the first speeches of Walpole,

Canning, Erskine, Grattan, Disraeli in the House of Commons failures? Were not the first works of most of our modern writers politely declined with thanks? Success! What is success but the triumph over past failure? *Mon ami*, if you have never been a fool, you will never be a wise man; if you have never failed, you will never be successful. The best across country are not those who have had the fewest falls.

Mortified at his failure, Jimmy vowed that he would court Imagination no more; and, with a sneer, said he would leave that sphere 'to the women.' It is astonishing how savage were his reviews on all the novels that crossed his path at this time, and how highly moral were the reproofs he directed against the frivolity of the public taste. Certain social topics then being discussed, Jimmy took the matter up, infused his humour and classical culture into the question, and wrote a few letters signed 'R. S. V. P.' to that great journal the *Trimmer* upon the subject. They were inserted, and led to his permanent engagement on the staff. His letters, with the signature 'R. S. V. P.,' on international law, penny ices, cheap divorces, gamekeepers' fees, domestic economy, justices' justice, tips to servants, state of the nation, state of Rotten Row, model farms, baby-farms, what to do with your manure, what to do with your poor—in short, on anything and everything, were regarded by the public mind with the respect and consideration accorded only to the epistles of the most brilliant writers of the day, which occasionally, through the medium of the *Trimmer*, kindly advise the estates of the realm how to act, the law-officers of the Crown how to legislate, the bench how to decide, and society generally how to behave.

For the next few years Hugh Lister led the ordinary life of the literary man-of-all-work. He wrote reviews on books of all classes—from an encyclopædia to an Oriental grammar—by studying the preface and deriving his information from the pages he criticised, then winding up with praise or abuse, according to the state of his liver and the bother the volumes gave him. He wrote essays, pamphlets, magazine articles, a book of travels, which was read and forgotten, and edited a classical author. It was at this time that he painted the head of a cardinal, which he fancied was, for shade and colouring, worthy of Rembrandt. As I have said, it was not accepted by the Royal Academy. One member of the hanging committee, as he examined it, said he was prepared for anything from an English artist, but he must really draw the line at sign-boards. Genial and good-tempered as are naturally most burly men, it is a sure 'draw' to get Jimmy on the subject of Art. His ire is hot and his invectives unbounded when he dilates upon that close borough, the Royal Academy. As Liston imagined that tragedy was his *forte,* so Lister sneers at his literary fame, and thinks that the brush and not the pen should have been his calling, and that he should be handed down to posterity, not as a Fielding, but as a Raphael.

So some fifteen years passed away since Hugh Lister quitted the cloisters of Alma Mater. Beyond the literary circle in which he lived he was almost unknown; his friends recognised his talents, and wondered why he had allowed his intellectual inferiors to distance him in the race of life. Great things had been anticipated from him by all in his set, still he had not realised the expectations formed of him. Men not worthy to clean his inkstand were drawing their hundreds from the publishers and were household names at the libraries, whilst he was still grinding away at journalism and hack-work. At last the hour came, and the man was found ready.

Whilst fishing in Scotland, Hugh Lister was laid on his back with rheumatism. Immured in a little Highland village, unable to stir out, free from the excitement of society and the interruption of friends, as he slowly recovered he bethought himself of a story, and began for the second time to write a novel. His experience of life had matured; he had always been a keen observer of character; his sense of toleration had deepened; his powers of sarcasm, humour, pathos, had widened in their range and increased in intensity. He took Balzac and Fielding as his models; he wrote leisurely and thought much; two years he spent over his work, and then gave it to the public. The time had not been wasted. The book was one exactly suited to the cynical, genial, religious, infidel, ostentatious, retiring spirit of the age, and its success was unbounded. It dissected character, especially female character; it laid bare the selfishness of human nature; it lashed the vices of society and held up the mirror to the world, so that it saw itself, not flattered or distorted, but faithfully reflected. We love to be told of our faults and virtues, especially when we attribute all the virtues to ourselves and burden our neighbour with the faults.

The future of Hugh Lister was assured. He was the Balzac of the day, and anything from his pen found a ready market. Since his first venture he has written numerous works, some good, some bad, some indifferent, but all commanding a large sale and handsomely swelling their author's banking account. A great man is Jimmy now. He dines with dukes and bishops; he lectures in America; he is a member of several learned societies; he takes the chair at literary meetings; he is a member of far more distinguished clubs than the

Caravanserai; he has declined a seat in Parliament; he is said to be worth a small fortune. When I read Jimmy's books and wince under his satire and caustic cynicism, and then see him at the club, his fat sides shaking with laughter, his hand ever ready to help a friend, always generous, kind, and good, it strikes me what a difference there often is between what a man *writes* and what a man *is*. I wonder whether 'goody' authors in their private lives are acid, spiteful, and stingy? Satirists are often the pleasantest of fellows; but may it be forgiven if I say that moralists and the 'gushing' fraternity have occasionally been found far from agreeable society? We all of us have a certain amount of spleen to get rid of: the literary cynic vents it on paper, the literary gusher on his friends. Which do you prefer?

Whilst at the zenith of his prosperity Hugh Lister resolved to carry out an idea that he had long meditated. As most actors are ambitious of developing into managers, so many men who have been engaged in journalism are desirous of being at the head of a newspaper. Lister thought he saw his way to start a new organ, and being well supported by a few sanguine peers of the Moderado party, and by three or four wealthy City men, began to put his scheme into execution. The journal was to be conducted on certain novel principles.

It was to be written by gentlemen for gentlemen; private secretaries were to communicate what official information they could impart; men thoroughly in society were to give the tittle-tattle of the day—gossip which could be relied upon and not contradicted in the next number; the leaders were to be written by the best brains that money could buy; foreign correspondents were to receive the salaries of ambassadors, and furnish the latest intelligence from the capitals to which they were accredited; the dramatic, literary, and artistic criticisms were to be in the hands of men who had been encouraged by success, and not soured by failure, and who were to have no crotchets or personal animosities; the City article was to be intrusted to a firm of such wealth and position as to render it like Cæsar's wife, above suspicion; the ladies were to be propitiated by articles on the fashions direct from the workrooms of the great Paris men-milliners themselves; whilst hospitality was to be encouraged by the proprietors of the journal giving every fortnight magnificent 'breakfasts' at their offices to the illustrious and the fashionable of the London world.

During the winter months the proposed newspaper was fully talked about in society and at the clubs, and well ventilated by the press. Early in the season the first number of the *Piccadilly Courier* made its appearance. Its success was never one moment in doubt. It was so well printed, and on such charmingly-toned paper, that the blind could almost read it. It was so well informed on all the subjects of which it treated, that to doubt its accuracy was like doubting infallibility. On all sides it had friends; never did a journal steer so cleverly between extremes without running aground or shattering its circulation by bad editorial navigation. The aristocracy liked it because it was properly deferential to privilege and prerogative, and held a right view (that meant an aristocratic view) upon the land question, game-laws, and all vested interests. The middle classes liked it because it took a just view (that meant a mercantile view) upon all commercial subjects, and advocated freedom in trade, general progress, and the most complete toleration. Pious people liked it because it was Catholic without Popery, and Protestant without Dissent. Worldlings liked it because it was witty, cynical, and epigrammatic in its observations upon men and manners. Society generally liked it because it told it exactly what it wanted to know without being cruelly malicious or impertinently inquisitive. The 'breakfasts' were a most successful institution, and ladies fought over the possession of cards as they fight over anything which is new and the rage. In short, the *Piccadilly*

Courier at one bound placed itself at the head of journalism, had its claims allowed, and has since declined to be ousted from its proud position.

And now it was that Hugh Lister became a great personage in London society, and was christened Jimmy. It was said that he knew everything, could 'make' anybody, and was in the most intimate confidence of the Cabinet and the Royal family. He was a lion in club smoking-rooms. He went to all the great parties in the season, and to all the great country houses in the autumn. He had his portrait painted—not after Rembrandt—and hung in the Academy. When he walks out or rides in the Row people nudge each other and say, 'See that fellow? that's Lister, the great novelist and editor of the *Piccadilly!*' He is one of the sights of London, like the Monument or the Tower. Yet wealth and fame and flattery sit very well on him. Success is like wine—some men it exhilarates, some men it makes sulky, some it does not affect. Jimmy is of the last order. Prosperous, celebrated, fêted, he is the same joyous, genial, epicurean being that he was when he was working his steps up the ladder of fame.

Rest on your well-won laurels, Jimmy, most stanch of friends and cheeriest of companions! Long may your brain teem with its present fertility, and never may you Swift-like 'wither from the top'! Long may the charms of music delight you, the little dishes you love—alas, too well!—nourish you, the drama amuse you, tobacco solace you, and the life you so thoroughly enjoy be preserved in all its vigorous completeness!

It will be a sad day for those you leave behind when your burly form is missed, those chatty lips silenced, and that joyous, hearty, unmusical laughter heard no more. Ay, and it will be a sadder day to the struggling author you have so generously befriended, to the unknown actress whom your praise has encouraged to further efforts, to the wearied reporter, the worn-out press-man, and to the whole community of the sick and afflicted, when you have been summoned hence, and have joined the majority. But why talk of the urn and the cypress? *Non omnis moriar.* In the hearts of your friends you will always live, and when they cease to beat Literature will enshrine you amongst her favourites, and jealously guard your name for posterity.

THE CLUB.

THE CLUB.

During the last generation a great domestic revolution has been gradually taking place, which promises to effect no unimportant changes in the constitution of English social life in the latter part of the nineteenth century. As a people, we have been so long accustomed to pique ourselves upon the strength of our domestic affections, upon our more solid characteristics, and upon our devotion to the attractions of our own fireside, that in spite of circumstances somewhat calculated to dispel this national belief, we still wrap ourselves in our superior virtue, and congratulate ourselves that we are not as our neighbour. We still vaunt the sanctity of an English home, and with a sneer at the freedom of continental habits, pronounce the word to be untranslatable. We still view with pity the benighted 'foreigner,' who, ignorant of the fascinations of a pure, a bright, and a cultivated home-life, prefers in their stead the gossip of his café or the whist of his *cercle*, and think if he but crossed the Channel and studied our manners and customs how valuable might be the lessons he would receive. Here, in our respectable country he would see the *home*, that word for which his language has no equivalent, taking the place of external dissipation, and the household gods so warmly worshipped, that it would be deemed iconoclasm of the most ruthless character to depose them from the pinnacles on which they are set. Ah, happy England! where your houses are so well built that your citizens are never tempted to quit them; where thoughtful servants attend to your every order, and give a dignity to the office of service; where your young women are so prudently reared that the most perfect house-discipline inevitably follows in the wake of marriage; where your young men, unselfish and industrious, are content to begin as their fathers before them began, and to wait till success has attended their labours before exchanging a severe economy for a graceful extravagance, and where all is nobleness of purpose, improvement of mind, and modesty of conduct. Ah, thrice happy country! What need for a Utopia so long as she exists!

I am afraid, however, that there is something unsound in this pæan of self-praise. It requires only the slightest amount of national introspection to find that we are not so different from our neighbour. Boast as we may of our superior tone of morality, the difference is but slight between London and Paris, London and Vienna, or London and St. Petersburg. With us secrecy and modern honour are now synonymous terms—'Do what you like, but be not found out,' is our maxim—and we conceal much which our neighbours expose. Thus we are more discreet; but discretion is not morality. We may vaunt our love of home-life as we please, but there are very strong indications that such love is fast loosening its hold upon us. Great wealth, a long peace, the popular position occupied by trade, the rapid removal of the social barriers that used formerly to exist, have all succeeded in bringing us to the not very enviable condition described by Wordsworth:

> 'Our life is only dressed
> For show: mean handiwork of craftsman, cook,
> Or groom! We must run glittering like a brook
> In the open sunshine, or we are unblest:
> The wealthiest man among us is the best:
> No grandeur now, in nature or in book,
> Delights us. Rapine, avarice, expense,
> This is idolatry; and these we adore:
> Plain living and high thinking are no more.'

But of all the circumstances that are tending to cause English life to enter upon a new phase of existence, none is more powerful or more insidious than the establishment of the modern club. Fifty years ago it was the exception for a man to belong to a club. The fact of club-membership then implied some social position or distinction on the part of the individual. White's,

Brooks's, Boodles's, and a few other establishments, constituted the palaces in Clubland, and to obtain the *entrée* was a matter of no little difficulty. A man of humble birth, or one unknown to the committee, would have been sure of being blackballed. Clubs were then filled by those who belonged either to the same political party or the same fashionable coterie, the members of which were all known more or less to each other. The Tory patrician entered himself at White's; the Whig politician of good blood was a member of Brooks's; the country gentleman put his name down at Boodles's; the distinguished lawyer, divine, or man of letters, became a member of the Athenæum; the soldier who was a field officer crossed over to the United Service; whilst the *roué*, the rake, and the dandy punted at Crockford's. Save as a house of reunion, in which to write letters and to play high, a club in the past was of little service to its members. A club was then an exclusive circle, not a restaurant. Men visited it, they did not live in it.

But now, owing to the development of the wealth of the country, the spread of education, and the easier condition of the community generally, a great change has taken place in the kingdom of Clubland. When the advantages of that coöperative system, based upon debentures and supported by entrance fees and annual subscriptions, which we call club-life, became to be more fully appreciated, it was found that the demand exceeded the supply. In all the old-fashioned clubs the books were so crowded with names, that almost half a generation had to elapse before a candidate stood his chance of election. The only solution of the difficulty was to found new clubs. One by one, as years rolled on, the little shops in Pall Mall and St. James's-street were demolished, and on their ruins rose stately edifices such as Venice in her palmiest days would not have been ashamed of owning. New political clubs, new professional clubs, new social clubs, sprang into existence, till what was a luxury in the reign of George IV. is now a comparative necessity.

Except at one or two establishments, which have always been reserved for those of recognised position, no man, provided he does not commit the unpardonable sin of keeping a shop (but as many warehouses as you please), and there be nothing known against his character, need despair of being a recipient of club favours. If he be blackballed at one institution, there is little to prevent him from putting his name up at another. His father before him had but a limited choice; whereas he, the son, can try his chance at several. Is he a Tory, but his blood not blue enough for White's—the father of the club system—he can still seek admission into the Carlton, the Junior Carlton, the Conservative, or St.

K

Stephen's. Is he a middle-class Whig, and fearful of being 'pilled' at Brooks's, what is to prevent him entering his name at the Reform or the Devonshire? Does he belong to one of her Majesty's services, his choice is embarrassing, for the list of naval and military clubs has recently been largely swelled. Still, what with the two United Service Clubs, the Army and Navy—more popularly known as the 'Rag'—the Naval and Military, and the East Indian United Service Club, 'an officer and a gentleman' ought to have little difficulty in getting quarters at one or other of these establishments. The officers in the Household Troops, however, make a coterie of their own at the Guards' Club. For the University man who hails from classical Oxford or mathematical Cambridge (Dublin, Durham, and the like need not apply), there is the choice between the University Club, the Oxford and Cambridge, or the New University Club. For the distinguished divine or lawyer, *savant* or man of letters, there is the Athenæum, whilst for the actor, the literary man, and the man about town, the Garrick opens its hospitable doors. To him who does not wish to bind himself to any political party, but seeks a *cercle* of a purely social character, there are the Travellers', Boodles's, Arthur's, St. James's, the Windham, the Union, and for Anglo-Indians the Oriental, of curry celebrity. The Marlborough is for the friends of the

Prince of Wales. The Park, the Badminton, and the Turf are the favourite haunts of the man of pleasure. The Portland is sacred to whist. In addition to this tolerably full list, there are a number of other clubs less well known, where the subscriptions are lower, and where the rights of membership can be claimed without any delay. At the accession of George IV. there were but some half-dozen clubs; there are now close upon a hundred.

It is impossible that this increase in the club-system should have attained to its present height without affecting the current of English life, and altering the course of its stream. A brief comparison between the past and the present will show the nature of the change that has taken place. In former days, when Pall Mall and St. James's-street were crowded with the shops of tailors and of bootmakers, instead of the magnificent palaces that now occupy their site, men led a very different life from that now in vogue. A buck, a macaroni, a Corinthian—the 'swell' of the past—lounged into his club to write a letter or to take a hand at whist, and considered such an institution as an indispensable adjunct to the character of a man of fashion—as necessary as a knowledge of French, or to be a connoisseur of china or of old fiddles. But to the ordinary man, born in the ranks of the middle class, who had to look to a profession for his livelihood, a club was out of the question. The young man reading for the bar, the younger son in a government office, or the merchant's son in his father's counting-house, had to content himself with tastes and habits in accordance with his income. He lived in modest lodgings or in chambers on the third floor of one of the Inns of Court. He dined off the joint at a tavern in the neighbourhood of Covent Garden, and it was with him a red-letter day when he ordered a pint of wine. When he went to the play he patronised the pit, and even on such occasions took advantage of the system of half-price. He seldom entered society, partly because it was expensive, and partly because he was not frequently invited. When he lounged down Bond-street or walked in the Park, he considered himself a dandy of the first water, and the anxiety he evinced as to his dress, and the extreme *hauteur* of his swagger, plainly proved that his promenade was an event not to be lightly considered, nor one of frequent occurrence. If he was a sensible fellow he worked hard at his profession, and looked forward to the day when he could complete his modest career by matrimony. Solitary lodgings, tavern dinners, an absence of comfort, there was little in his life to make celibacy desirable, and marriage was the haven for which he steered his bark. Thus, as soon as his income justified him in taking that important step, he married. If the parish registers of the earlier half of the nineteenth century be examined, it will be found that more than two-thirds of the marriages that then took place were entered into before the bridegroom had

reached thirty. This is a fact which should not be lost sight of by the social historian.

But if we turn from the past to the present how different is the picture! The continued prosperity of the country in spite of the increase in the cost of living has greatly benefited every class in the community. The lower orders receive higher wages and are better off than their fathers, whilst the incomes of professional people have more than doubled themselves. The introduction of a plutocracy among the aristocracy and the acreocracy, though it has tended somewhat to vulgarise our social institutions, has succeeded in developing a rate of expenditure which formerly did not exist. Money easily made is lavishly spent. Never was there a time in our history when heavier rents were demanded by the house-agents, higher prices by the horse-dealers, more exorbitant sums by carriage-builders, milliners, breeders of stock, jewellers, tailors, by everybody in short who ministers to the wants and luxuries of man. Since wealth enjoys now the power and advantages formerly possessed by high rank and high intellect, display has assumed the position of a social force. We give better dinners, ride better horses, live in better houses, drive about in better carriages, yet all not so much for the sake of the enjoyment of excellence, as for the exhibition of the pride of rivalry.

The consequence of this plethora of wealth has been to create throughout the community fictitious and artificial tastes. The customs and fashions of our fathers have been deemed capable of improvement. Quarters that had once been fashionable have been gradually deserted.

The glory of Bloomsbury and Baker-street has departed, and Belgravia, where, amid its swamps at the beginning of the century, men shot snipe, and South Kensington, once noted for its market-gardens, are now the districts favoured by the great world, and by those who wish to be thought within its circle. The old taverns of the Strand and Fleet-street, and the neighbouring regions, have given place to joint-stock hotels, where everything, including the wines, is brand new. The dinner-hour has become later and later, till to 'dine in hall' is like dining in the middle of the day. The young lawyers and students having found no advantage in living near their Inns, but, on the contrary, that they are far removed from the scenes of social dissipation, migrate to the west, quitting Lincoln's Inn, the Temple, and Gray's Inn, for the dingy back streets in the vicinity of St. James's. The long peace had caused the army to be dull, so that men as soon as they obtained their companies retired as a rule from the service. Thus it was, what with a large population of idlers, and an increasing luxury all around, that the advantages of the club-system began to be seriously considered. Men wished to have comfort without extravagance, and attendance without responsibility. It was known that the clubs that had come into existence at the accession of George IV. were in the most flourishing condition, and that their members had all the advantages of an exquisitely appointed house without the expense and trouble of proprietorship. One by one, as it became more and more difficult to be admitted into the older establishments, new clubs sprang up, and have continued springing up, till now Clubland, from an exclusive and limited territory, has developed into an extensive and densely populated domain, offering hospitality to all who have the slightest claim to that somewhat elastic title of 'gentleman.'

With the establishment of the club-system a great revolution has taken place in the domestic life of men, and especially of young men. Married men, accustomed to the refined and luxurious mode of existence in a club, endeavour, so far as their means will permit, to reproduce its elegance and perfections within their own homes. They send their cooks to have a fortnight's training under the eye of the superb club *chef*; in their appointments of the table they imitate the club; their wine-merchant is often one of the fraternity who supplies the club; and to say 'they could not dine better at the club' is to confer the highest praise upon one's domestic arrangements. It was in the year 1850 that the club-system became popular, and that the club, from being a lounge, developed into a home. Let an elderly man hark back in his memory, and compare the dinners to which he was invited before the Crimean War, and those to which he is now asked, and he will find that the superiority of the one over the other is due not a little to the host having been educated by his club.

But it is in the life of the bachelor that the introduction of clubs has caused the greatest change. The solitary lodgings and the tavern dinners have been relegated to the limbo of the past. All that is now needed is a bedroom, for the club provides the bachelor with the rest of his wants. It matters little in what dingy street or squalid quarter a man lodges, for the club is the address, and society inquires no further. He need not purchase an envelope or a sheet of note-paper throughout the year, for the club provides him with all the stationery he can possibly require. There is no occasion for him to buy a book, a magazine, or a newspaper, for in his club he will find a library such as few private houses can furnish, and in the morning-room every newspaper and weekly review that has a respectable circulation. Does he wish to practise economy without privation, where can he dine better and cheaper than at his club? If, on the other hand, his tastes are those of a *gourmet,* and his income permits him, where can he better satisfy the cravings of a cultivated epicureanism? Both to the social Dives and the social Lazarus the club is a boon. The poor man enjoys life without the discomforts that ordinarily attend upon poverty, whilst the rich man receives to the full the value of his money.

To that large class which is neither rich nor poor, the club is a most cherished haunt. A young man on some four or five hundred a year enjoys advantages at his club which only the wealthiest outside can command. For an annual subscription, after having paid his entrance fee, of some eight or ten guineas a year, he finds himself part owner of a most splendid town house, where the tax-collector never intrudes, where repairs and dilapidations never concern him, where attentive servants wait upon his every order, where everything provided is of the very best, for it is worth the contractor's while to give satisfaction, where retirement can be obtained without the depressing sense of solitude, and where companionship can be enjoyed without the dangers of intrusion—in short, a home always well appointed, always bright, and ready to cater for the simplest necessities or the most elaborate luxuries.

One of the most prominent consequences of all this perfection of organisation has been to render celibacy so desirable, that matrimony, instead of being the natural ambition of man, is now regarded by many in the light of a sacrifice. To marry, unless on an income which is the exception, signifies the exchange of club-life, with its pleasant gossip, its agreeable luxuries, and all its disciplined requirements, for the monotony of the domestic hearth, the worries of housekeeping, and the servitude of family restraint. Under the old order of things, when clubs were the exception, matrimony was regarded as the panacea for all the ills that bachelordom was heir to, and a man married in order to have the companionship of a home. Whereas now, in that one word *club,* men find a safer substitute for the uncertain advantages of matrimony. 'Why should I marry?' asks the celibate. 'What are the advantages that marriage will bring to counterbalance its disadvantages? At present with my income I am well off, the club supplies me with all my wants, and my movements are unfettered. If I marry, I descend at once to be a poor man, with all the mortifications and privations of poverty. The charms of marriage are all very well, but what if they be followed by anxiety, by boredom, by disappointment? Such has been the fate of many; why should it not be mine? Even in a happy marriage there must be a vast amount of monotony.' That this selfish and one-sided reasoning is daily gaining ground amongst us is evident from the decrease of marriages, and the increase of the club-system, not only in London, but in provincial towns.

I know no better illustration of these views than my friend Tommy Montague. An ex-cavalry officer, who was compelled to send in his papers from certain financial circumstances over which he had no control, the future of Tommy was not particularly bright. An allowance of 150*l.* a year granted him by a surly elder brother, and the proceeds of his commission, could hardly be considered a state of affluence for a man who had never made himself acquainted with the value of money, and to whom self-denial was an unknown virtue. As fortune would have it, one evening, at a certain set of chambers in the mansion of the Albany, Tommy had such a run of luck whilst playing *écarté* with a young peer who had just come into his possessions that my lord preferred, instead of mortgaging some of his acres to obtain the necessary ready money, to allow Montague for the rest of his natural life the annual sum of five hundred pounds, to be paid quarterly by his lordship's solicitors. Tommy had no objection to the arrangement; and from that very hour up to the present time he has never touched a card; he is one of the very few who have made gambling pay, and he is quite content.

On this annuity, coupled with his brother's allowance, and the interest on the money he received for his commission, Tommy leads the quiet luxurious life of the club-man who spends his all upon himself. Tommy's maxim is that money spent upon oneself is never wasted. A garret in Bury-street is the only *pied-à-terre* he owns, for the club to him signifies lodgings, restaurant, country house, library, divan, —in fact, home and all. He hates sport, travelling, and society, and prefers the club in August and September to anywhere else without the club. To see him really wretched you must watch him when his beloved haunt is shut up for repairs, and he has either to go out of town or to betake himself to a strange club which has offered him hospitality. On such occasions he is thoroughly miserable, for it is not club-life that Tommy merely loves, but the life of his *own* club. He likes to breakfast at the same table, to read the newspaper in the same chair at the same window, to write his letters at the same table, to study the bill of fare at the same accustomed stand, and to have his dinner served by the same waiter at the same corner of the coffee-room. He is the strictest and most monotonous of Conservatives. Never was there a man whom it is more easy to find. You know the hour to a moment when he breakfasts, when he takes his 'constitutional,' when he smokes his first cigar, when he lunches, dines, writes his letters, reads, and goes through the programme of his thoroughly selfish but not uncomfortable life. He seldom enters society, and, with the exception of running down to Brighton or Folkestone for a fortnight, never visits the country. The club is his home, and save to take his daily stroll or to go to the theatre, of which he is very fond, he hardly stirs from its walls.

He is the great critic of the establishment, and we all feel that our comfort is safe in his hands. If the slightest thing goes wrong in the club—the ventilation imperfect, sanitary arrangements out of order, waiters inattentive, books missing, newspapers forgotten to be taken in, and the like—dip goes Tommy's pen in the ink, and the secretary is at once informed of the fact. At the annual meeting Tommy is a perfect Joseph Hume. He is irritatingly inquisitive as to every detail of club expendi-

ture, and declines to be content with the brief statement in the circular issued by the committee. He wants to know why there should be a loss on the coffee-room, why so much should be spent upon snuff, toothpicks, and stationery, why the bills for repairs should be so enormous, why the salary of the secretary should be raised, why so little is added to the sinking fund, and all the rest of it. Nor will he be put off with a smile from the chairman, or with a little bit of flattery from some of the committee. He wants to know the reason why; and when Tommy 'wants to know the reason why,' the information he seeks must be lucid and complete before he is satisfied.

He is the terror of the club-servants, and backs his bill remorselessly if the joint which is down for eight o'clock appears half an hour late, or the wine-butler makes a mistake about the vintage that is ordered, or the waiter at his table is not perfect in his duties. Tommy knows to a day when everything is in season, and woe betide the steward if at the earliest moment there are no plovers' eggs, no asparagus, no green peas, or no new potatoes! He is acquainted with the price of every article, and instantly checks any attempt on the part of the club to overcharge its members. He is the great authority on club discipline and club etiquette; but everything outside the club he views with supreme indifference. Talk to him of some awful disaster, of some terrible commercial failure (provided he be not affected by it), of some great national loss, of the death of some great man, and his interest will hardly be excited; but tell him that the excellent club cook has given notice, that a certain bin of rare wines has been drunk up and cannot be replaced, that the hall-porter has broken his leg, that there has been a 'row' between certain members on the committee, or that Brown has not paid his debts of honour, yet still persists in sitting down to whist, or that the member who steals the umbrellas has been caught in the act, or that Jones has been declared a bankrupt, and what will be the action of the committee, and you at once find him a ready and suggestive listener. The club, the whole club, and nothing but the club, is the one creed of Captain Montague.

A hard selfish man, *à l'âge de la gourmandise*, the Caravanserai provides Tommy with all that he requires. He declines to dine out, because he says he gets a better dinner at the club for some ten or twelve shillings than at the best houses in town; and why, he inquires, should he bore himself with dull society when he can have the chat and ease of the smoking-room? If he wants to be amused he goes to the theatre; if he wants to be instructed he goes to the library: what has he to do with society, he asks with a sneer; he has no money, and he has not a pretty wife. He is perfectly content with the future before him, and as he makes his bed so has he no objection to lie upon it. In spite of shaving off his whiskers, cutting short his moustache, and freely using a wonderful hair-dye, Tommy is not the young man strangers would at first sight take him for. Quiet, comfort, good living, freedom from responsibility and anxiety, are the great desiderata of his life, 'and, begad, you don't get that by

marriage!' he remarks. Talk to him of the solicitude of a tender wife, of the charms of home, of the soothing power of affection during the feverish hours of a long sickness, and he answers, 'O, of course! but I get all that from a nurses' instiootion; two guineas a week and beer-money.'

To convert Tommy is hopeless. He will never be made to see that he leads a purposeless selfish existence, occupied with petty details, making a business of trivialities, and ignoring all that is great and noble in life. He will dine and chat and moon the days away till the sands of the hour-glass are all run out, and the hearse stands before his lodgings to convey him to that great club which is open to us all, and from which no black balls exclude—the cemetery. Then the blind of his room will be pulled up, somebody else will sleep in his little bed, there will be a few allusions during the next fortnight in the club he loved so well to 'poor Tommy,' and then—well, then he will be as completely forgotten as if he had never been. Yet Captain Montague is under the impression that were he to quit the club it would at once fall to the ground. Such is the difference between the estimate we form of ourselves and that formed of us by other people.

M. F. H.

M. F. H.

WHATEVER faults the present day may possess, from the one great vice which is generally attendant upon a luxurious state of civilisation it is happily free. We may be all that the cynics and satirists allege, but from one grave accusation we are at least exempt—the courage of Englishmen is as high and daring as it ever was. No poet of the future, as he tunes his lyre to sing of the men and manners of the nineteenth century, can give vent to the bitter sneer of Horace, as he wailed over the degeneracy of the Roman youth:

> 'Non his juventus orta parentibus
> Infecit æquor sanguine Punico,
> Pyrrhumque et ingentem cecidit
> Antiochum Annibalemque dirum.'

In all feats of pluck and prowess the young Englishman heads the list of the adventurous. On the Continent his eagerness for unconventional excitement, and his contempt for danger, have caused him to be branded with the stigma of insanity. Nothing is too extraordinary, nothing is too arduous, nothing is too perilous, for the 'mad Englishman' to undertake. He ascends mountains that even the local brave flinch at scaling; he will scull his outrigger, or paddle his canoe, in the most unknown and dangerous of waters; he will cross the most boisterous seas in the pettiest of yawls; he will betake himself to the wildest regions to satisfy his cravings after sport. The fact that a certain event has never before been accomplished is alone sufficient to tempt him to undertake it, and to give him no rest till it has been brought to a satisfactory termination. In all these feats of daring he seldom has any great object to serve which justifies the peril that is to be encountered. The excitement of danger, and the desire to find a vent for his wealthy supply of nervous energy, are in themselves often the only inducements which lead him to enter upon his self-imposed tasks. I remember once talking to a young Englishman in Switzerland, who had just come down from making the ascent of one of the severest and most seldom climbed of Alpine peaks. 'What a splendid view you must have had from the top!' said I. 'They say there is,' he replied quietly; 'but I never looked at it. I don't care for views.' The exercise, the fun, and the peril were all that interested this athletic young Philistine.

But there is one sport which of all others is essentially English, which is first favourite amongst us, and which want of money is the only reason that prevents it from being freely indulged in by all classes. There breathes not an Englishman who does not, provided his banker's book sanctions the expenditure, take to hunting as instinctively as the duckling takes to water. The horse is the special object of our national veneration. Your ordinary Englishman is not much hurt if his grammar or spelling be found fault with, but he is wounded to the core if his riding is condemned. He does not pretend to be a connoisseur in the fine arts, he admits that his taste in wine may want educating; but will he ever forgive you if you tell him that he is no judge of the noble animal? He will, as a rule, bear kindly much hostile criticism, but he is the touchiest of mortals where his stud and his seat are concerned. This sensitiveness is perhaps the strongest proof we have of our innate passion for the chase. Since hunting is our great pastime, and the breed of our horses the finest in the world, it becomes almost a reflection for an Englishman not to be able to sit his fences or to express ignorance upon the points of a horse. However modest he may be, there are two things an Englishman always piques himself upon—he can ride, and he is a judge of horseflesh. You may doubt his parentage, his fortune, his ability, ay, even his honour; but if you doubt his possession of these two gifts you have made an enemy who will never forgive.

In comparing the past with the present, there are few things which more strike an elderly man than the new phase hunting has entered upon. That it is a sport which has always been a favourite with us is evident; but it was never so popular or so generally indulged in as at the present day. Thanks to the increased wealth of the country, and to our being able to use the railways as our cover hacks, hunting is brought within reach of most of us. The well-to-do idle man will always have his hunting-box, or take up his quarters at a well-known hostel in the neighbourhood of the meets; nor is there now any necessity for the man in active employment—the barrister, the merchant, the banker, and the like—either to give up his sport or his business; such an one can combine both: he can work in the City, and yet, by the aid of the friendly locomotive, have his two days a week. I know one hard-working lawyer in town who, though among the most industrious of his fraternity, yet hunts regularly his two days a week; he keeps his horses at Rugby; the North-Western is his cover hack; and thus, without detriment to the interests of his clients, he is able to enjoy in moderation the sport he so dearly loves. In former days this was impossible; men who hunted were then within easy reach of the hounds they followed; now several of the best subscribers to a pack live at a considerable distance from its neighbourhood.

Thus hunting no longer appeals especially to those who reside in the country, but comprises both the rural and urban populations. How many men engaged in our manufacturing towns hunt regularly through the winter, who, before the introduction of steam, would have been compelled by the necessities of their pursuits to abandon the sport altogether! This is no doubt one of the chief reasons why so many more packs of hounds have come into existence than were known of at the beginning of this century. And it is a good sign. Hunting is a test of courage, of endurance, of activity, of health, and of all those qualities which call forth presence of mind and quickness of judgment; and it speaks well for the manhood of a country where such a sport is, as it is amongst us, so enthusiastically encouraged. Of course in every field there is the 'coffee-housing' sportsman —his hat, his natty tie, his well-cut coat, his spotless leathers, all that the hatter, the haberdasher, the tailor, the breeches-maker, and the boot-maker can show of superior workmanship; who has a perfect knowledge of the local geography; who declines to jump the slightest obstacle, but who is acquainted with every gate, gap, and bridle-path which will eventually bring him up with the hounds; and who after dinner, when the decanters are making their pleasant rounds, will gallantly talk of the brooks that he cleared, the posts

and rails that he leaped, and the doubles that he so
cleverly took. In pleasure as well as in business
there are impostors; but as a rule the fault of our

young men is, not that they funk, but that they ride
too hard.

There is one member of the Caravanserai whom it is
always a great pleasure for me to see within its walls.
Among the 'hard riders of England,' Ashby Folville, the
popular master of the Slottesloe foxhounds—one of the

levellest, best-looking, and fastest packs in the country—holds a prominent place. Bad at his books, he is one of those men who excel in every kind of manly sport. Though now past forty, there are few young men who do not own themselves vanquished by him, where gun or rifle, rod or spear, tennis-ball or cricket-ball, is concerned. Sport is the only atmosphere he breathes or cares to breathe. I know no one to whom an accident which would render him a cripple for life would be more intolerable. Rob him of his enjoyment of physical exercise, and you deprive him of all that makes existence delightful. When Folville is not hunting or shooting, he is salmon-fishing, sculling, cricketing, mountaineering, or in some other form getting rid of the superfluous energy with which he is so abundantly blessed. But good man as he is all round, it is to the king of sports that he swears the most ardent attachment. What the meeting of Parliament is to the ambitious legislator, what the first day of term is to the lawyer, what the beginning of the season is to the beauty, is the first Monday in November to the jovial squire of Highthorpe Abbey.

And small blame to him, as the Irishman says. In the whole round of pleasure is there any excitement more intoxicating, is there any exercise more health-giving both for man and woman, is there any better training for the acquisition of courage, than hunting?

It is the only innocent pleasure which never palls upon us. The early rising and the anticipation of the day's sport give us an appetite such as all the tumblers of medicinal waters can never excite. As

we ride to covert, Nature, clad in the russet hue of early winter decay—like a woman, Nature never tries to please so much as when her beauty is on the wane—offers us vistas of sylvan scenery, views of down and dell bathed in the morning dews, and studies of clouds which stimulate all that is of the artist and of the poet within us. Conversation is never so easy and so brisk as when we meet at the cover-side, smoking our last cigar before the business of the day begins, and criticising the mounts of our friends and the fair faces of the women who enliven the scene by their presence. Then the pause of expectation, and the encouraging pull from our flask, whilst the hounds are drawing the cover; the deep long-drawn-out note proclaiming a find, the chorus of the pack, and away we follow; our first fence taken, confidence is restored, and we are ready to hold our own with the wickedest. In the excitement of the run, the light south-west breeze stirring the air around us, the scent breast high, the pack running really fast, our mount full of heart and go,—at such a supreme moment we know nothing of physical ills, we ignore all the anxieties that have been oppressing us; disease, debt, care, misery, are thrown off with the hounds; and for one day, at least, the wicked cease to trouble us, and the weary are at rest.

The sport never loses its interest. When gout or rheumatism compels us to exchange the saddle for the phaeton, like the ruined gamester, whose greatest delight it is to hover round the fatal board of green cloth, to watch the fall of the cards, and to speculate as to what colour or number he would back, though he is powerless to stake a farthing, so we who are invalided are always ready to drive the ladies to the meet, to pass our comments upon the hounds and the horses, to have a friendly chat with the redcoats ere they start, and to see as much of the sport as the line the fox takes and a knowledge of the neighbouring roads will permit. It is true there is another side to the picture. A lame horse, miles away from anywhere, our flask empty, our sandwich-case lost, our coat and leathers wet through, a sharp penetrating rain, night and a sore throat coming on, and a terrible march to the nearest station from which we can box home. Or the crashing fall, the gate taken off its hinges, which serves as the impromptu stretcher, the darkened room, the weekly six guineas from the 'Accidental' till we recover,—or perhaps we may never require that pension. In all sports there is a certain amount of danger; but this we maintain, that when we consider the number of men who ride to hounds, and compare that number with the accidents which occur during a season, few will admit that hunting is the dangerous pastime its enemies allege.

If the noblest study be man, I am sure the noblest specimen of his race is an English gentleman. He is courteous, yet manly, which your foreigner so seldom is; he is proud, yet not haughty—proud with the proper sense of self-respect; he has a large stake in the country, and he is conscious of it; he comes of a line that has been gentle for centuries, and he is not ashamed of the fact. He may be a profound scholar, or he may have only enough learning to examine the accounts of his steward, to say a few words without breaking down at an agricultural dinner, and to take his seat amongst his brother magistrates without disgracing the bench; but where will you find honour more unsullied, hospitality more generous, and truth more loved for its own sake than in the order to which he belonged? England, in spite of her climate and the diatribes of her critics, is his ideal of all that a country should be. Whatever be the creed he professes, or the political principles to which he adheres, neither his religion nor his party is permitted to interfere with his patriotism. He is an Englishman first—a disciple or politician afterwards.

Ashby Folville is no bad type of his class. In tastes and sentiments he is a thorough Englishman. He thinks there is no country like England, for in no country, he says, can you spend so much time out of doors. For beauty and wholesome surroundings he considers his own fair countrywomen as first, and the rest nowhere. When he travels he is amused with the foreigners he comes across, though he never fails to regard them as an inferior people. In his opinion there is no man out of England who can ride; or handle a team without coming to grief; no man but an Englishman who has an idea what real sport is; no gentleman like an English gentleman, and no pluck like English pluck.

The face and figure of Folville are eminently English. Though he rides well-nigh sixteen stone, his height, the broad powerful shoulders, and the mighty limbs take off from the appearance of his bulk, and make him look a lighter weight than he really is. His face, with its healthy complexion, gives signs of the outdoor life he so dearly loves, and were it not for the finely-cut features it would not escape the stigma of coarseness. I suppose he has his cares, yet they must sit lightly on him, for the keenest observer fails to detect worry on that bright open countenance. To watch him cheering on his hounds, to hear his jovial laugh, to listen to his simple honest talk, are all as good as change of air to the bilious and the acrid. Yet that well-shaped mouth of his can give tongue to pretty vigorous expressions should a young farmer head the fox, or ride over a favourite hound. If a man be heir to a good name, if his fortune be ample, if his health be sound, and if he have brains enough to carry him through his ordinary duties, but not brains enough to make him ambitious and discontented, life, let the moralist preach as he may, is to such a one full of enjoyment from find to finish.

The possessor of one of the finest seats in the country, happily married, rich, well-born, the squire of Highthorpe Abbey has little cause to grumble at his lot. Genial, generous, hospitable, he is the first M.F.H. who has hunted his country to the satisfaction of its neighbourhood. Before he took over the Slottesloe hounds, incessant were the squabbles in the district; master after master had succeeded to the command of the pack, yet had always come to loggerheads with the subscribers; the farmers wired their fences, and breathed threatenings and slaughter against all who dared to ride over their land; petty spites were at work, and permission was often refused for neighbouring coverts to be drawn; the pack deteriorated; there was no lack of foxes, yet no sport could be got; and at last the question of selling the hounds was seriously discussed.

At this juncture Ashby Folville stepped in. He had just succeeded to the paternal estates, and to a father who was as fond of chemistry as the son was of sport. He agreed to take over the hounds. He took a pleasure in their working and management, and he would pay keepers, stoppers, damage, everything, himself. Need I say so liberal an offer was gladly accepted? Young, wealthy, and known to be a venturesome rider, the country soon rallied round him. What was denied to crabbed elderly men was granted to him.

Neighbouring landowners sank their jealousies; the farmers were won over, and became the most ardent of the supporters of the hunt; and gorse covers, where the woodlands were deficient, were judiciously planted. At the end of four years the number of hounds reached sixty couple, boasting some of the best blood from the finest kennels in the kingdom.

Slowly but steadily the fame of the pack increased. Hunting-boxes in the neighbourhood were let at double their former rents. A large joint-stock hotel, with the most extensive stabling, was erected at Highthorpe. Men came down from London with their horses to hunt with the Slottesloe, as they went into the shires to follow the Pytchley or the Quorn. The name of 'the squire' became as a household word in the sporting circles of the country. Mounted on his powerful brown horse, it must indeed be a quick thing which fails to see Folville close up at the finish. In spite of every obstacle that falls in his way to negotiate, he can tell you the name of every hound that was leading during any part of the run; he has an eye for country such as few cavalry officers possess; his ear, never at fault, tells him in an instant the course his hounds are taking, and when sound is useless as a guide, he seems to have an instinctive knowledge of all the turns and dodges the fox is up to. It is not therefore surprising that when its master shows such sport 'the Slottesloe' should be a great favourite with all who can and dare ride, and that the right to wear the uniform of the hunt (olive green with buff facings) should be much coveted.

Every November finds me invariably a guest at Highthorpe Abbey. Both the squire and his charming wife know the art of hospitality to perfection. As a rule, most country houses are very enjoyable from the hour of dinner to the end of the evening—pleasant people, well-dressed women, a good table, the produce of favourite bins, conversation, music, billiards, whist, and the wind up in the smoking-room, form a combination of delights which cannot but please even the most difficult. It is the early part of the day which is often such a trial at many country houses. Can there be anything more depressing than that awful meal of breakfast at several houses? It is served punctually at half-past nine, and your host regards it as a slight upon himself if you do not put in an appearance. You have sat up late, you are nervous, you are irritable, you have no appetite, you want to have your cup of tea and bread-and-butter in bed, and wait till your letters arrive. Yet you are bound to talk and be agreeable, and take an interest in the children, and be as lively as if you were at dinner. There is no meet anywhere in the neighbourhood that day, and perhaps the weather does not tempt you to go out shooting. People have been invited without any regard to each other's tastes and habits. You think one man looks like an actor and that you will have some fun, and you find he is a missionary. You essay to get up a flirtation with a pretty girl, and she will have none of it, but bores you with questions upon scientific subjects of which you have never heard. The few pleasant people in the house are always in their rooms writing letters. You propose a game of billiards, but the only man who can play got up at seven in the morning to ride twenty miles to cover. You wander into the library, but there are no modern novels, and you care for no other kind of literature. The host is engaged his own way; the hostess is engaged hers; girls you would like to know have formed themselves into little groups, and you fear to intrude. And so you end by mooning down to the stable with one or two friends equally bored with yourself, to smoke. Some people think when once they have invited you to stay with them, that they have done all that is required, and you must amuse yourself as you best can. To make country-house life agreeable, you ought to be able to afford either excellent sport, when a man will accommodate himself to dull society and indifferent cooking, or if the sport that you can offer be only moderate, your house should be filled with pleasant people, and the cunning of your *chef* a thing to be fondly anticipated and gratefully remembered even by a Catius. At Highthorpe Abbey the visitor has little cause to grumble. The house is always full during the

winter with charming married women, pretty girls, amusing men, and with one or two celebrities in art and literature to give a tone to the conversation at dinner and to assist the ladies in their sketches or in the solution of acrostics. If you feel lazy after the severities of the past week, you tell the comely Hebe who brings you your morning cup of tea that you are not going down to breakfast; and accordingly a fire is lit in your room, your *déjeuner* is served up-stairs, and, being in the bachelors' wing, you can smoke, write your letters, or read the country papers without intrusion. At Highthorpe you have all the ease and independence of an hotel with all the charms of a gay and luxurious country house.

A strong bond of union exists between the host and his visitors. Everybody in the house rides, and is devoted to hunting. The Squire hunts his own hounds four days a week, and you are within an easy ride to cover of the Brookby Holt harriers and the Revesby and Hawthorne foxhounds. If the visitor at Highthorpe be a glutton, he can hunt his six days a week, so far as hounds are concerned. Everything is redolent of the pleasures of the chase. Walking along the corridors of the old house, at every turn you come across valets, either taking to, or bringing from, their masters tops, leathers, and pink or black coats. The end of your chamber's bell-rope is ornamented with a fox's brush, your inkstand is a fox's head, and the handle of your paper-cutter a fox's pad. Over your mantelpiece, side by side with the cards that tell you of the arrival and departure of the London trains and the hour when the post goes out, is a list of the meets of the Slottesloe and of the neighbouring packs. When you go down to breakfast (no formal long table, but little tables scattered about the room, at which you can be as sulky or

as sociable as you please) you see ladies in their habits —the cut and fit plainly suggestive of hard riding— and the men in all their bravery of pink, or in Melton coats and gorgeous waistcoats. Talk to them of Patti *la Diva* or of Thalberg *la petite*, yet to most of them there is no music like the deep-throated chorus of the pack, or even of the tramp of the hoofs of the horses as they are being brought round.

Yet, enthusiastic as all the inmates of Highthorpe are about hunting—if you do not hunt you will be about as cheerful there as a salmon on a gravel walk— it is the rule of the house that during dinner all hunting topics are to be strictly tabooed. As you take your tea in the library with the ladies before going to dress, you may talk about the run and the fences you took or the 'croppers' you came as much as you please; you may resume the subject when you adjourn to the smoking-room; but during dinner, and for a couple of hours afterwards, you are not to pose as the one-idea'd man, whose powers of conversation are limited entirely to the subject of fox-hunting. It is a most excellent rule, and, when we remember the mendacity and monotony that so frequently characterise this kind of talk, one well worthy of adoption. It does not follow that because a man is fond of hunting he is necessarily incapable of anything better. Some of the most distinguished men on the bench, in the senate, the camp, the studio, in literature and in science, have been enrolled in the ranks of the hard riders of England. Nor, on the other hand, is it a proof of intellect or humanity for a man to run down hunting. One of the dullest and savagest of critics that it has ever been my misfortune to meet is as sentimental as a schoolgirl over 'the poor fox;' but give him a book to review or a picture to criticise, and where is his charity, his tenderness, or his humanity? It has been expended upon the sufferings of hunted vermin, and is exhausted when he has to deal with his fellow-creatures. Ah, my bilious friend, take a few lessons in riding—even have a day with the Old Surrey—and your invigorated system will soon teach you that all who differ from you are neither so utterly in the wrong nor so hopelessly idiotic as your jaundiced imagination conceives.

Shortly after his arrival at Highthorpe, one of the first duties that the visitor—if he belong to what is ironically called the sterner sex—has to perform is to inspect the kennels and the stables. Skirting the well-timbered park, and pausing occasionally to watch the red and fallow deer feeding beneath the beech-trees, clothed in all the golden glories of their autumnal garb, our destination is soon reached. The kennels and stables at Highthorpe are a fine range of buildings, erected at no little cost by the Squire, and freely supplied with water which is pumped up by steam to an elevation commanding the whole of the buildings. The first-whip's house is close to the kennels; and many a vicar is worse lodged. After a rigid inspection of the dog-pack and the 'ladies'—it is best not to hazard a criticism if your canine knowledge is deficient, for there are few better judges of the points of a hound than Ashby Folville—brought out on the sward for your express benefit, and having had the young hounds drafted out for special examination, you are nothing loth — for perhaps you have been nervous as to the calves of your legs—to be taken over the stables. The stable-yard consists of a wide square. On one side is a covered riding-school; on the opposite side is a magnificent range of loose boxes; on the third side is an equally magnificent range of stalls; whilst on the fourth side are the boiling-houses and meal-stores. Men are never shy when invited to Highthorpe about asking leave to bring down their horses, for room can always be found for them; whilst, on the other hand, he who has no horses can easily be accommodated with nags; for the Squire's stud is an extensive one. 'If you can ride I can mount you,' says Folville to the young men who come down from the University to spend their Christmastide with him. However, he would not give his dearest friend leave to lay his legs over certain valuable animals at the north end of the stable, which constitute the Squire's own lot. When a man pays from three to five hundred guineas for his hunters he is justified in being selfish.

When a frost sets in, or during a couple of months in the season (chiefly spent at Lord's), the Squire turns up frequently at the Caravanserai, preferring the gaiety of that establishment to the sedateness of Boodles's. He knows everybody worth knowing in the club; and we to whom he has been civil in the country do our best to repay his hospitality. When Mrs. Folville gives a dance, and though she is not a fashionable dame as the London world counts fashion, we of the club take care to send her a strong contingency from our best waltzing division, so that there shall be no lack of good partners. Her little people are always being taken to the play; indeed the governess has remonstrated more than once, as these attentions, she says, interfere with the studies of her charges. When her boys get an *exeat*, and none of the family are in town, there are always plenty of us glad to receive the lads, and to send them on their way rejoicing with a tip. As for me, I am always charmed when it lies within my power to make any return for the hospitality and kindness it has been my good fortune, winter after winter, to receive at that pleasantest of country houses—Highthorpe Abbey.

CULTURE.

CULTURE.

Looking back at the past from the vantage-point now, alas! of many years, there are few features in English life which more impress me than the giant strides made within the last generation in the matter of National Education. The knowledge which was considered highly creditable in a young man when our fourth George was king would be considered at the present day as hardly worthy of the position of an intelligent City clerk. In those 'good old times' a man obtained his degree often without examination, or when he had to go through that ordeal his papers for 'greats' were scarcely superior to those now put before the candidate at matriculation. If the army was to be his career, he donned his Majesty's uniform without troubling himself about the Commentaries of Julius Cæsar, the epochs of history, or the course of English literature; his commission had been paid for, and nothing more was needed. Had he relatives in the law, he was destined for the bar, ate his dinners, and became entitled to wear his wig and gown, thanks to his stomach, and not to his brains. Was he a younger son with interest, he was appointed to a clerkship in a Government office, without first having to pay his fees to a crammer. But now the days of privilege are numbered, and the reign of Education has been ushered in. The creed of the survival of the fittest is the religion under which we live and move and have our being, and it must be admitted that the impecunious born fool of this our age has a roughish future before him.

Yet it is an ill wind that blows no one any good. If the lot of the noodle is a hard one, that of the clever man was never more brilliant. Patronage has given place to competitive examinations, and the world of official and professional life is no longer an exclusive area, but an open field, where the prizes of the race fall to the swiftest. The scholar has it all his own way. He does not require to come of an ancient line, or to know a Cabinet Minister, or to possess capital; all he needs to command success are brains,—with perhaps a baptismal or medical certificate. He can rise to the highest posts in the service of our Indian empire without being the nephew of a director or the friend of those in power in Downing-street. He can wear the blue of the Artillery and the scarlet of the Engineers; he can fly his flag as an admiral; he can take his seat on the woolsack; he can wear the lawn sleeves; he can become a member of the Cabinet—there is no limit to his ambition but the throne and the grave, provided he be one of the brilliant pupils of our new schoolmaster. As Demosthenes extolled the advantages of action, action, action, so now the sires of the rising generation din into

the ears of their sons the advantages of education, education, education. Can we therefore wonder that the temple of Minerva should be thronged with worshippers? A great statesman once wrote that we lived under the Venetian system. Under whatever system we lived before the first Reform Bill, there can be little doubt about our now living under the Chinese system.

Nor is this progress in education limited to the higher classes. Culture—I believe that is the correct word—is now the aim and desire of all save the most vagabond. What with endless cram, competitive examinations, mechanic institutes, popular science, and text-books on all subjects for the million, it will be quite a treat in a few years to meet with a man who knows nothing. A veteran like myself, educated under the old *régime*, is about as much at home in modern conversation as an alderman upon a penitential diet. Everything that I learned in my youth has to be unlearned. Historical characters that I was taught to regard as monsters are now proved to have possessed every domestic virtue; whilst the men who appeared to me all that was noble and good have, alas, turned out to be villains of the blackest dye. The constant revelations of science—and science is a subject which was never my strong point—bewilder me to exasperation; for no sooner have I made myself familiar with a recent discovery and disabused myself of all my former prejudices, than some great leader of science starts up, and proves most satisfactorily that what I have just acquired is nothing more than a tissue of false conclusions drawn from unsound premises, and utterly worthless in theory and in practice. Then this enlightened person is in his turn contradicted by another great leader in science; and so the ball goes rolling until, what with dogmatic assertions and vehement refutations, it seems to me that life is too short to make a study of science. It is the same with theology: all my early impressions upon the subject have been shown to be most erroneous; yet what to believe is very puzzling, for no two divines teach alike, and every theory is at variance with its fellow.

Sometimes I think the ignorance and simple faith, which were the fashion in my younger days, preferable to this very advanced state of education, which destroys so much and builds up so little. We are so educated that not only do youths in their teens glibly discuss the most abstruse subjects, but our lower orders have caught the contagion. They in their turn have acquired that little knowledge which Bacon says is so dangerous a thing, and the consequence is that they are gradually becoming discontented with their position in life. The educated tradesman is ashamed of keeping a shop, so he calls his quarters an 'emporium.' The working man, who jumbles up history, geography, and political economy at a night-class, calls himself an 'artisan.' The counter-jumper, who drops his *h*'s at a debating-club, dubs himself an 'assistant.' The bagman is a 'commercial gentleman,' the young person is a 'young lady,' the clerk is an 'employé,' the hairdresser is an 'artiste,' and for aught I know to the contrary the dustman may call himself an 'artiste in refuse,' and his brother of the watering-cart an 'employé in hydraulics.' A system of education which renders a man happier in his position in life, which makes him a better creature and a more respectable citizen, is a great national boon; but a system of education which makes him ashamed of his calling and sullen to his superiors, yet does not render him qualified for a superior station, is, it seems to me, a very doubtful advantage.

Hence one of the results of this false shame is to cause a great exodus from the working classes into the middle classes. The prosperous shopkeeper declines to bring up his son for the lower walks of trade. The field is now so open—thanks to the example set us by John Chinaman—and the prizes to be obtained by the highly educated are so worth the winning, that every one wishes to qualify for the race. The son of the yeoman and the son of the tradesman jostle the son of the gentleman at every step—at the public schools, at the universities, and at the great examinations. But though the prizes are many, the competitors are to be counted by their thousands; and as only the few can win, the many who are defeated have no alternative but to add themselves to the already overcrowded middle classes, and intensify the fierce fight for life. With those whom education has placed in the ranks of the victors, existence is no doubt pleasant enough; but with those who have not been so successful, who have tried and have failed, what is their future! How many a tradesman, who sees his son, of whom he had such expectations, plucked for India or the Engineers, getting no practice at the bar, obtaining no patients in medicine, discontented, idle, and fit for nothing, too good for trade, yet not good enough for anything else, must have regretted the day when he vowed 'he would make a gentleman of the boy' instead of sending him into the shop! And how many a son, suspicious and sensitive, and made perhaps by an unkind world to smart under his social shortcomings (you want money and success to carry off *some* things), must often have felt, in spite of his 'position as a gentleman,' that it would have been better for him to have been as his father before him, a prosperous tradesman, than a poor and unsuccessful 'gentleman'!

One man whom I know within the walls of the Caravanserai must often have indulged in such reflections. Mr. Thorne can hardly be considered in the light of an eligible member of our community. We are told that a little leaven leaveneth the whole lump, and it is surprising how disagreeable one cantankerous man who uses his club can make it to those around him. He is always coming upon the scene and cannot be avoided. If you go up to the library you find him snoring on the very sofa you want, with the very book you have come in search of in his useless grasp. If you dine accidentally at the club your table is sure to be placed next to his. Are you having a quiet chat with a friend in the smoking-room, most assuredly will this wretched being drop in and spoil the conversation. He is always quarrelling with the committee, and asking you to support his complaints; nor is it a pleasant task to refuse the requests of the cantankerous. At billiards he disputes the accuracy of the marker; at whist his frowns and reproofs intimidate his partner; if you turn up the king at *écarté* his expressive smile plainly conveys to you the impression that he considers you a swindler.

From these observations you will perhaps gather that Mr. Thorne is not a popular personage, nor in arriving at that conclusion will you be much mistaken. Indeed, he is not a favourite. There are some men, no matter how illustrious their birth or how high their office, who from their charm of manner and attractive geniality are always known to their fellows by some fond *sobriquet* or affectionate diminution of their Christian name; but who, looking into the pale spiteful face of Mr. Thorne, with the sinister set in his cold gray eyes, and the angry lines round his snappish mouth, would ever think of addressing him otherwise than as Mr. Thorne? He has no friends, and the list of his acquaintances is limited.

When he speaks to you he draws himself up to his full height, regards you with elevated eyebrows, and a general look of lofty superiority on his sickly countenance, and expects you humbly to listen to him, as if he were conferring a great favour in imparting the opinions his splendid intellect has arrived at to so incompetent a creature as yourself. 'What I hate about that fellow,' said a frank youth to me, 'is that he always treats every one as if he were a damned ass.' The remark is forcible, but it not inaptly hits off the character of this superior person.

Mr. Thorne is one of those men with whom conversation is impossible. He will address you, he will lecture you, he will instruct you, but he will not chat with you—conversation with him is a monologue. He is to preach, you are to listen. If you interrupt him he will look at you as if utterly dumbfounded by your audacity; if you advance an opinion he will promptly contradict it; and if you ask him a question upon a subject of which he knows nothing he will reply in his nastiest tones that 'he is not a schoolboy.' When he is present he is Sir Oracle, and permits no one to interfere with his monopoly of eloquence and information. He passes his judgment upon the works of the greatest writers, patronising them if he approves of their views, or running them down to the lowest depths of disparagement if he differs from them. The range of his criticism is wide, embracing every subject, from music to archæology, and from astronomy to comparative philology. Provided you are submissive and deferential he will answer the queries you put to him. Should you, however, hold views of your own, he will decline to enter into a discussion with you. 'I object to have my brains sucked,' he says loftily. As for me, I scarcely ever like to inquire after his health for fear he should think I want to 'suck his brains' about anatomy.

Quack is a favourite word of Mr. Thorne's. If a man has attained to fame by some brilliant discovery, or by the publication of some erudite work, or by the achievement of some great deed, Mr. Thorne, who hates success as only the failed can hate it, brands him as a quack. Essentially a critic, and the turn of his mind purely receptive, our lofty genius piques himself upon his creative faculties, and is indifferent to everything that is not what he considers original. It must, however, be admitted that there are few things which Mr. Thorne considers original outside his own literary efforts; for no sooner is some discovery said to be new, or some author becomes famous for the novelty of his opinions, than this kindly person proves that the discoverer has only improved upon an old plan, and that the writer is a plagiarist. Listening to this critic it would appear that we have amongst us no scientific men worthy of the name, no profound philosophers, no statesmen who are not adventurers, no historians who are aught than ignorant copyists, no artists, actors, engineers; in short, that there is in this country but one man whose learning and brilliant abilities save her from contempt, and his name is Mr. Ebenezer Thorne. If to detract from the fame of established reputations, if to take the exact opposite of public opinion, if to be guided alone by the spiteful views of a splenetic egotism be originality, no one will deny that Mr. Thorne is of all men the most original; and long may the monopoly of such a gift be confined to him!

The existence of such a creature is due entirely to our system of advanced education. Mr. Thorne is one of the painful results of culture—to be pronounced, if you please, 'culchaw.' The son of a fairly prosperous bootmaker in Oxford-street, he was sent as a lad to one of the large City schools. Here his aptitude for mathematics and the superior calibre of his abilities generally attracted the attention of the head-master. Young Thorne soon worked his way up to the sixth form, and gained most of the prizes in the school. It had been the intention of the worthy bootmaker to let his son have a good commercial education, and then to take him into the shop as a partner. But the father, like many men whose sons are more brilliantly endowed than themselves, was somewhat in awe of his boy. How could he ask a young man who could spout page after page from the orations of Cicero and Demosthenes, who could read the comedies of Molière without a dictionary, and who was quite at home in conic sections and hydrostatics, to add up a ledger, put on an apron, and take orders? There was no alternative but for the father to 'make a gentleman of the lad.' He came to this resolve with a

sigh, for he knew the profits of the shop were not to be despised; and, from several of the bad debts he had on his books, he also entertained a shrewd idea of what a 'gentleman' was. Yet there was no help for it; he had educated his son above his position, and there was little blame to be attached to the boy if he sneered at his father's calling. 'There is nothing like leather,' we all know; so let us appreciate at its proper value the sacrifice made by the parent.

Accordingly, young Thorne was sent to Cambridge. That he would pass all the examinations was never for one moment to be doubted. He had been the head of his school, and it was fully expected that he would greatly distinguish himself. Nor would these hopes have been disappointed had the peculiarities of his temperament not made themselves now painfully visible. Mr. Thorne declined to follow the counsels of his tutor; he rejected the books he was told to study; he disputed many of the conclusions that the greatest mathematicians had arrived at. His was one of those lofty minds not to be fettered by tutors and nourished upon school-books. He would rely only upon himself; he would take nothing for granted; he would be his own mathematician, geometrician, and astronomer; and the consequence was that instead of being, as he had modestly expected, Smith's prizeman and among the first three wranglers, he came out in the middle of the Junior Optimes. Of course it was from no fault of his; he had often feared what the result would be; the examiners were jealous of him, and had entered into a conspiracy to defeat him. One of the most painful features in the character of Thorne is that he never will acknowledge himself worsted from any failure of his own. As the Frenchman, when he is beaten, always cries out, '*Nous sommes trahis*,' so Thorne always ascribes his unsuccesses to jealousies, combinations, and conspiracies. Why the world should put itself to such inconvenience as always to spy upon his every action and misinterpret his every motive none of us have as yet been able to discover. Perhaps, after all, it may be that the world is not so malicious as Mr. Thorne alleges, and that its censures are but the outcome of its honest judgment and opinions.

Quitting Cambridge, Thorne took up his abode in London at the paternal villa of Fulham. So superior a person declined to go through the drudgery of working for professional success. He had no interest at the bar; he despised commerce; and of course, as became a man of his enlightened views, he held that religion was but the result of hereditary prejudices, and the Church an organised superstition. He resolved to devote himself to science, and to show the world how unjust had been the treatment he had received at the hands of that school of a larger growth—the University. He wrote a work on 'Gravitation,' in which his views were so 'original' that he inveighed against everybody who had previously illustrated the Newtonian theory, and maintained that his own conclusions were the only sound ones upon the subject. The book was damned by the press, and the publisher's ledger displayed an alarming sale of forty copies, of which twenty-five had been bought by the proud father of the author.

Still the confidence of Mr. Thorne in himself was not damped; the world only cared for frivolity, the critics were a parcel of venal and spiteful hacks, and the council of the Astronomical Society had conspired to crush him. He declined to be crushed. He wrote a volume on the 'Multiple Stars,' another on 'Sound,' a third on 'Tidal Investigations,' an essay on 'Optics,' and a treatise on 'Statical Couples.' None of these great works having succeeded in bringing either money or fame to their illustrious author, the old bootmaker roundly declared to his son that he could no longer afford to keep him in idleness, and that he must look out for some employment. A third-rate insurance office being in want of an actuary, Mr. Thorne sent in an application, and was glad enough to be appointed to the post. We have to thank one of his directors for electing this great genius a member of the Caravanserai.

We are told by Sydney Smith that the dissenters of Bicester were very fond of declaring that until their arrival there was no such thing in their town as intellectual light—all was wrapped in ignorance, incapacity, and the Established Church. Mr. Thorne is gifted with not a little of the conceit and arrogance of the Bicester dissenter. Until his election to the Caravanserai, he considers that no man of real culture or superior attainments has ever been admitted within the club. Though surrounded by statesmen, distinguished lawyers, well-known members of the House of Commons, men of letters who have taken high honours at the University, *et hoc genus omne*, he calmly regards himself as the one intellectual star of the establishment. It is his judgment that should alone be accepted; his opinion that should alone carry weight. He knows what the Government is going to do and what it should do better than the one or two Parliamentary Under-Secretaries who honour the smoking-room with their presence. He lays down the law about art, in spite of the R.A.s and A.R.A.s who are amongst his audience. If the Astronomer Royal were to sit at the next table to him he would condemn many of his conclusions. He criticises everything and everybody, yet in all his criticisms his object is to show, either by implication or by positive statement, how very much better he could have done the work under discussion. His own brains are the standard by which he measures everything; and therefore, whenever he says in his most dogmatic manner, '*I* cannot understand it,' or '*I* have never heard of it,' it is to be at once concluded that the subject which engages our attention is either too ridiculous or too trivial to be noticed. Whenever any classical or French quotation is made in his presence he has a disagreeable trick of asking what you said, and on the request being complied with of dryly saying, 'Oh!' and then of repeating the quotation *very* distinctly, as much as to say *that* is the way it should be pronounced. It was of Mr. Thorne that it was once remarked that had he been present at the Creation he would have given a few hints.

Yet, let us be charitable; for much of this irritating omniscience Mr. Thorne has a certain excuse. He has never found his level. At school, at the University, in his little circle, he has always lived in a set who have looked up to him with blind adoration. At home he is surrounded by those to whom socially and intellectually he is greatly the superior, and he lords it over the parental circle with that despotism which is generally accorded to these dictators of a coterie. Thus he has acquired a habit of not only laying down the law, but of imagining that because education is a novelty to himself and to those in his own sphere, it must be equally a novelty to others. We know how the man to whom champagne is an unwonted luxury talks about that vintage; how the snob swaggers about having met a lord; how the beggar behaves when set on horseback; and therefore we must not be hard upon Mr. Thorne, considering his shortcomings, that he somewhat over-estimates his erudition.

Nor has any one the wish to be hard upon him, if he would only act with a little more tact and modesty.

Conscious that he is the social inferior of almost every one in the club, he thinks it incumbent upon himself to assume a defensive tone in order to preserve his dignity. But he who is always on the defensive scarcely fails to be offensive. Suspicious to insanity, he snatches at every accidental remark, as if it were intended to convey a personal insult to himself. Should one member innocently say to another, 'It is ill waiting for dead men's shoes,' or 'There is nothing like leather,' or 'Shoemaker, stick to your last,' or 'What boots it?' or 'That is quite another pair of shoes,' and the like, Mr. Thorne grows pale and quivers, and imagines that allusions are being made to his origin. Of course at the Caravanserai we all know who the man is, though Mr. Thorne is under the delusion that he preserves the secret of his birth most cleverly; but with the good taste of Englishmen we do not permit ourselves to be prejudiced against him on account of any social shortcomings under which he labours, and willingly would we hold out the right hand of fellowship were Mr. Thorne a more agreeable personage. Yet with that strange inconsistency which is so puzzling a feature in human nature, it is Thorne who ever begins the aggressive; it is he who is always indulging in personal remarks, who is always branding a member as no gentleman, and who is always informing us what 'society' should do on certain occasions. It is true that he has more than once drawn upon himself some cruel retort which has silenced him for days, but it has only been after having richly deserved the punishment. He has made numerous enemies, and his foes know that his vulnerable point is 'the shop.' Thus tortured by his sense of social inferiority, yet exalted by what he considers his intellectual superiority, he goes through life transformed into that curious combination of antitheses which we so often see in men of the Thorne type—combative, yet shrinkingly sensitive; arrogant, yet humble; fearful of oppression, yet ever oppressing; a master one moment, a slave the next.

To me he is a study. Yet when I watch him turning pale at some covert sneer; jealous at the success of men who have distanced him; the holder of a petty appointment, after all the flourish of trumpets that had ushered him into the arena of life; bitter, sensitive, miserable—it seems to me how much happier he would have been had not 'culture' taken him out of his position, and we of the Caravanserai had been, instead of his companions —his customers.

FINANCE.

FINANCE.

THEORIES are like men, they may be crushed by scorn or ridicule; yet if they decline to be crushed they will end by being listened to, and by gaining followers. Looking over a file of old newspapers a few nights ago, and reading them by the light of some of 'H. B.'s' caricatures, I could not help comparing the present with the past, and reflecting how very different was the treatment which one peculiar theory met with in days bygone from what it now receives. Most of us can remember when the opinions concerning the 'Asian mystery' were first promulgated. We were told that mankind, instead of holding the Hebrew race in profound contempt, should reverence it for the important part it played in the history of the world. Without the Hebrew race, it was said, the records of Holy Writ would have been hopelessly lost; without the Hebrew race the creed of Christianity would never have been founded; without the Hebrew race the scheme of man's redemption would never have been accomplished. The Jews were both the favoured and the ostracised of the

Supreme Being; to their disloyalty as well as to their loyalty the world owed a deep debt of devotion.

We were told that the existence of the Hebrew race was a proof of its superiority over the other families of mankind. It had encountered the bitterest of persecutions; it had been dispersed; it had been oppressed by the harshest of laws; all over the globe it had met with cruelty, contempt, and infamous restrictions. Yet it lived, whilst the nations which had maltreated it had declined and had fallen, never to rise again. Not only did it live, but we were informed that, in spite of the awful past, the intellectual vitality of the Hebrew race was as vivid, as powerful, and as commanding as ever. Remove the shackles that fettered the Jew, admit him into the arena of life unhandicapped by the restrictions of intolerance, accord him all the civil rights of a subject, and speedily, it was alleged, he would work his way to the front, and stand a full head and shoulders above the rest of the crowd. From this fact it was argued we ought to learn a great ethnological truth—that a superior race cannot be absorbed or repressed by one that is inferior. Other races had existed as pure in their lineage as the Jew, but what had been their fate? Either they had been absorbed by their victors in intermarriage, or they had become extinct from the deadly thraldom of conquest. Save the Jew, there was not an instance in the world of a race, whilst subject for centuries to every evil influence that prejudice and persecution could suggest, having maintained both its purity of blood and its intellectual vitality. From this we were bidden to mark not only the fulfilment of prophecy, but the superiority of the Jew.

We can remember the wit and humour that were directed against this theory and against its Apostle. Yet the laugh has not been exactly on our side. The Apostle has proved the truth of his teaching in his own person, by a success which has never before fallen to the lot of a statesman in this country, whilst his theory is on all sides being most fully exemplified. Everywhere the Jew confronts his fellow-man, and stands forth as master of the situation. Admitted but yesterday to the bar, he is in the first rank of counsel, second to none in eloquence, in the lore of jurisprudence, and in the skill of the consummate advocate. The realms of finance have always been his especial dominion, but never has he occupied so powerful a position as at the present day; he holds empires in pawn, and by a wish to realise his possessions could reduce half a continent to bankruptcy. His civil disabilities removed, he becomes a legislator distinguished by his ready gift of debate, or a magistrate conspicuous for his tact and common sense. Music and song and the drama have been so eminently the monopoly of the Hebrew race, that no one is surprised at a great composer, or a great actress, or a *prima donna* being of Jewish descent. In art, in science, in literature, the Hebrew is again among the most gifted in his

profession. Whatever department is open to him, his success in it is so remarkable as to make him one of the conspicuous. When the field of his intellect was limited to medicine and finance, he rose till he could rise no higher; and now that the world closes none of its avenues at his approach, the talents which made him attain distinction when under persecution render every career he selects in this age of his toleration a brilliant one.

The Hebrew has all the qualities which lead men to prosperity. A keen brain, intense perseverance, great industry, great nervous energy, frugality, an ambition that never loses an opportunity, a conscience somewhat dulled by that cunning which is hereditary in the persecuted, pushing, active, knowing instinctively what to accept and what to reject,—it is not surprising that his success is marked. Between the Jew and the Scotchman—though both cordially dislike each other—there is much in common. Both comprise within themselves all that is good and bad in human nature in a marked degree; both clan together, seldom working singly, so that the success of one brings other successes in its wake; both carry their nationality in their face; both are eager after the main chance, and somewhat indifferent as to the means, provided the end be gained; both are frugal and persevering; both are imbued with strong religious prejudices—and both sold their king.

It is in society that the position of the Jew has become the most conspicuous. Men now not elderly can remember the time when the Jew was never met with at the houses of the great. He lived apart, formed a community of his own, and was regarded as a pariah outside the pale of social existence. A dame of fashion would have felt her self-respect wounded had she permitted a Jewess to enter her drawing-rooms, whilst a peer would as soon have asked a Jew to his country house as he would the hangman. But as wealth became more and more the idol of the age, as one by one the barriers set up by prejudice were uprooted, and as Judaism, gradually losing its distinctive characteristics, developed into a kind of deism, society had to march with the times and extend its frontiers. The Jew was admitted, and his tact soon transformed the bare inch which was reluctantly doled out to him into the lengthiest of ells. It is a curious fact that whilst the middle classes still entertain a strong prejudice against the Jew, nowhere is he more cordially welcomed than amongst what are termed the higher classes. Whether this is due to the fact that the more rarefied the social atmosphere the freer is it from the vulgarities of intolerance and the artificialities of civilisation, or that Hebrews, themselves strongly tinged with aristocratic sentiments, take more pains to please when in the society of the great than when amongst their equals, I know not.

There is one member of the Caravanserai to whom many of these remarks refer. It is now many years since Hermann Wertheim left his native city of Magdeburg to seek his fortune and build up a prosperous career for himself. Obscure, penniless, unbefriended, he began life dependent entirely upon his own resources. What the history of his lineage is none of us know, though, since he has attained to celebrity, malice and imagination have been busy with his name. Yet whatever his parentage may have been, there can be no doubt as to his Hebrew origin. There are various types of Jew. There is the low-caste Jew—bullet-headed, bull-necked, olive-hued, snub-nosed, with low brow, greasy curls, negro lips, and redeemed alone from the most forbidding ugliness by the splendid eyes of his tribe. There is the Jew in the humbler walks of trade, short, fat, and differing little from the physiognomy of the ordinary Frenchman save in the hook of the nose and the peculiar shape of the eye. There is the Jew whose wealth has raised him for generations above the common herd of his fellows—who is the aristocrat of his race—whose features are finely cut; the forehead broad yet lofty; the nose aquiline, and only when past middle age developing into the Judaic curve; the mouth, though too full, yet beautifully shaped; the chin firm and decided; the shape of the head, the ears, the hands, the feet, all showing unmistakable signs of breeding. There are dark Jews and fair Jews, red-headed Jews and bald-headed Jews, little dumpy Jews and tall slim Jews, Jews bearded like the pard, Jews shaved like priests; yet different as are these various types of Israelite, in the cast of countenance, and above all in the melancholy expression of the eyes, the ob-

server has seldom any difficulty in deciphering the nationality. Wertheim is a dark man with black curly locks, large brown eyes, an aquiline nose, and a long well-kept beard; he might pass for an Italian, were it not for that peculiarity of expression which stamps him at a glance as a Jew. By the women he is considered very handsome; the men say he would be good-looking were he not a Jew.

The career of Wertheim is a curious one. Whilst a

lad at Magdeburg he read an advertisement in an English journal stating that a firm of merchants were in want of a clerk. He thought the opportunity a good one for perfecting himself in the English language, and applied for the post. He was successful, and was engaged at the modest salary of forty pounds a year. At the end of three years he rose to the position of correspondence clerk. Here his knowledge of foreign languages, his shrewdness, his business capacity, his tact and foresight, caused him to be regarded as one of the most useful of officials. He was sent over to Rio Janeiro as a junior partner to manage the fortunes of the Brazilian branch of the firm. Before he was forty he had succeeded—thanks to the busy hand of death—in becoming senior partner, and then retired from the business, demanding as his share some two hundred thousand pounds.

With this sum Wertheim speculated largely in the United States during a season of great commercial depression, and well-nigh doubled his fortune. He now came to London, took splendid offices in the City, and soon established a reputation as one of the happiest of financial promoters. He touched nothing which did not dissolve itself into gold. Every company he brought out was a success, and paid handsome dividends. His name as chairman or director of a mine, a line of railway, a joint-stock bank, or any other financial association, inspired the public with confidence and sent up the price of its shares. His terms were heavy, yet speculators were only too glad to pay what he asked, provided he would promote the companies they proposed to him.

When it was known that Wertheim had consented to bring out a company, the competition for allotments set in fast and furious, and the shares once floated were bought up at a heavy premium. His offices were always crowded with eager capitalists anxious for an interview—not always granted—with the great man, imploring him to take their money and invest it in any undertaking he thought best. At first the great City houses looked somewhat askance at the 'adventurer,' as he was called; but they ended, as the rest of the fraternity had ended, by hanging about his magnificent anterooms and invoking his aid. It is better to be born lucky than rich, says the proverb; but when a man is both lucky and rich the ball lies at his feet. Wertheim was lucky. Numerous as had been the enterprises in which he had been engaged, none had been miserable failures, none had led to investigations which reflected upon his honour. Some were paying twenty per cent, some were only paying four, but there was not one of them at a discount. The official liquidator had never had occasion to intrude himself unpleasantly upon the presence of Hermann Wertheim. It was computed that within ten years he had realised nearly a couple of millions.

And now the self-control and sagacity of the man appeared. At the very zenith of his prosperity, when he was worshipped in the streets and lanes around the Exchange, when every continental Bourse was applauding his ventures and exaggerating his successes, when committees of the House of Commons listened to his opinions as conclusive, when he was looked up to both by the Treasury and the Bank of England as the soundest of financial advisers, Wertheim sold his offices in the City and retired from every undertaking in which his name appeared. Jews are, of all people, the most pleasure-loving and the least given to *ennui* or satiety. They drink the cup of life to the dregs, and find the last quaff almost as pleasant as the first. Wertheim had worked and won; he would give ill-luck no opportunity; the rest of his days he would pass in leisure.

A brilliant position east of Temple Bar signifies at the present day a brilliant position west of that now happily removed obstacle. Gradually, first through dandies and politicians who had sat with him at the same Boards of Directors, then through Ministers who had asked him for counsel, and then through certain great ladies of a speculative temperament, who had been indebted to the famous promoter for allotments, shares, and early information as to railway amalgamations, Wertheim entered society, and his wealth soon made him a personage in the circles of its leaders. It is difficult to understand how a race, shunned and oppressed like the Jews, should have obtained that social tact and power of pleasing, when it suits them, which are eminently their characteristics. There is hardly a capital in Europe, where a Jewess by her brilliant social gifts is not amongst the leaders of its society; and the Jew, whether he be one by religion or by blood, who has mixed much in the world, is always a witty and amusing companion. It is only when among his equals or inferiors that the egotism, the selfishness, and the lack of scruple of the Hebrew appear.

Hermann Wertheim was not only admitted into good society; he was soon courted by it. The women considered him handsome; his manners had much of the repose and dignity of the Oriental; his conversation was always amusing and could be instructive; whilst his wealth gave him that assurance and self-respect which other men obtain from high birth and acknowledged position. He bought a beautiful property in the favourite home county of his race, and one of the best town houses that the agents had on their books. He was unmarried, and such a *parti* was not likely to be permitted to remain for long unattached. Whatever creed Wertheim inwardly professed, he was to all intents and purposes a Christian. In the country he was a model squire, and from his large curtained pew in the village church repeated the responses in a most edifying manner. In town he could be seen every Sunday morning in the fashionable fane of his quarter. He had a few livings in his gift, and was most orthodox in the exer-

cise of his patronage. He took a great interest in the future of the English Church, and spoke once or twice on the subject at Congress meetings. Whether he was ever baptised no one inquired; he was for all practical purposes as much a Christian as half the inhabitants of the kingdom, and to look deeper would have been both impertinent and inquisitive. Still the Jews are an adaptive people, and in posing as a good Protestant Hermann Wertheim may after all be but an outsider in the fold. Wandering up Edgeware-road one fine September morning, I entered the splendid synagogue of that district. It was the Day of Atonement. Gazing at the sad sallow countenances of the worshippers, it struck me that I saw the great ex-financier in their midst. As our eyes met, he buried his face in his *talith*. Perhaps after all I was mistaken—one Jew is so very like another.

It took few of us by surprise when Wertheim married Lady Delia St. Julien. Everybody knew that the Earl of Leoville was as poor as poor could be, and that his clever wife had devoted the best part of two seasons to ensnare the capitalist. The match has proved a happy one for both parties. The mortgages on Medoc Castle and Romanee Park have been paid off, and the Countess has taken her diamonds out of pawn—I mean has received them back from her banker. Lady Delia—a dame of some five-and-thirty, very cold, very haughty, very distant, and who would have married Beelzebub, had she been assured of the extent of his rent-roll, to benefit her family—has come to the conclusion that she is a most fortunate woman. Domesticity has always been a marked feature in the Jewish race, and Wertheim is no exception to the rest of his tribe. Fond of his wife, passionately attached to their only child, he has succeeded in transforming Lady Delia from a statue into a most agreeable and charming woman. Thanks to the wealth and generous disposition of her husband, she has made her house one of the most popular in town. In the country their hospitalities are conducted in the most lavish manner. The house is seldom free from visitors; and as Wertheim is himself a splendid musician and somewhat of an artist, one meets there not only the fashionable, but the celebrities of the drama, the studio, and the library.

Considering that Hermann Wertheim is a man much sought after, he is a frequent visitor at the Caravanserai. He has many friends, especially amongst the young and the hard-working who have not yet attained to fame. At his dinners and Lady Delia's balls the youth of the Caravanserai show up in great force, whilst he places his stable and his shootings almost too much at their disposal. He has his enemies; but when they have called him 'a German Jew,' and sneered at him as an 'adventurer,' they have little more to say against him. Besides, he has been forced so frequently to meet these two charges during his life that their venom has long ceased to wound: he has found the antidote in wealth and success.

One regret he certainly experiences. Imbued with a sincere admiration for the institutions and the people of England, a naturalised subject himself of her Majesty, and well read in political history, he would give much of his bullion to be able to enter the House of Commons. Those green benches have an attraction for him which the promoting of companies or the bringing out of loans never possessed. When an important debate takes place he may generally be seen sitting behind a friendly member under the gallery. How slight is the barrier that divides him from the House! yet by him it can never be o'erpassed. As I see him watching speaker after speaker, the mere routine of the business of the House having a special interest for him, the desire of his heart can be read. He is another instance of a man not completely happy. He has wealth, he has talents, he has health, he has a delightful home; yet the one thing he yearns after he has not (had he it, would he yearn after it?)—the power to take an active part in the legislative labours of the nation of his adoption. Among those who have gained much, yet who still long after the unattainable, the name of Hermann Wertheim must also be written.

> 'Inde fit, ut raro, qui se vixisse beatum
> Dicat, et exacto contentus tempore vitæ
> Cedat, uti conviva satur, reperire queamus.'

WITS.

WITS.

THERE are few things more puzzling to the unsophisticated mind than the manner in which certain people, without any definite means of subsistence, manage to live. We know that such persons have no profession, that no kind relations have put their names down for handsome legacies, that they are social waifs and strays, not clearly belonging to anybody or to anything; yet they appear always to be amply supplied with the goods of this world, and freely to enjoy the pleasures thereof. If they are married they live in the most charming of *bijou* establishments, give excellent dinners, where the male element somewhat predominates, drive in the easiest and most miniature of broughams, ride the cleverest of hunters in the shires and the most perfect of hacks in the Park, and are always to be met with in the haunts that Fashion specially selects for her amusement, and everywhere maintaining a rate of expenditure of several thousands a year. How do they do it? We know that the husband was 'broke' in the Goodwood of

18—, and that his wife had nothing; how, then, do they exist in comfort and splendour?

On the other hand, if they are bachelors they give their address at one or two good clubs, they are clad in

purple and fine linen, and fare sumptuously every day. They have their stall at the Opera and their hack for the Row, they are not content with the club points at whist, but bet heavily, and they always have money to entertain useful friends at the neatest of little dinners, and to gratify the sins they most affect. Yet how is it done? We see men with good fortunes, making a lucrative practice or holding high and well-paid appointments, and yet they say candidly that they should come to signal grief did they launch themselves forth on the lavish career which is the daily life of these penniless puzzles. Again we ask, How do they do it? The answer returned is, By their wits.

At the present day the clever impecunious adventurer finds many an active sphere for his peculiar labours which was denied to his predecessor. In the olden times our friend, whose keen wit had to stand him in the stead of lofty name and handsome revenues, was forced to open the world with his sword as a soldier of fortune, or to ingratiate himself, under the happy feudal system, with a monarch who would offer him the requisite facilities for marrying an heiress, or else to descend to the tricks and cunning of the downright knave. He could punt over the green cloth at games of hazard, it is true; but your man who has to live by his wits can seldom afford to play unless he has a decided advantage over his opponent; he is willing to keep the bank, to play whist or *écarté;* a game of skill is an income to him, whilst a game of pure chance defeats his calculations and renders his superior knowledge valueless.

But in these easier later times there are numerous roads and convenient bypaths which lead to the temple of Fortune—the temple of Honour is behind the temple of Fortune. A knowledge of horseflesh can in itself be employed so as to gain a comfortable annuity; a crack 'gentleman jock,' though he is disqualified from getting his three pounds a mount and five pounds when successful, may yet make an excellent thing of his riding, thanks to the little investments put to his credit by his employer. And as for the income that can be obained from whist, from *écarté*, from billiards, from pigeon-shooting, and from making a book on the different races, it may vary according to the capital and capacities of the 'sportsman,' from one hundred to thousands a year. The man who has to live by his wits, provided he be not ashamed of the profession and his nerve and talent fit him for the career, need scarcely nowadays grumble at the opportunities afforded him for distinction—and perhaps for notoriety. There are plenty of pickings for the rook; the fox seldom prowls about in vain; and the fold is so feebly guarded that the wolf now almost wants a whet for his appetite. The creed of the survival of the fittest is an excellent arrangement for the fittest; to those, however, who are not in that category it is perhaps open to objection.

Among the predatory individuals who are especially

created, as it were, to live upon their fellow-men, Davie Benson will always occupy a prominent place. No one knows who he is, what his parentage is, what locality gave him birth, or what his available means of subsistence are. He is the child of mystery, nor does he ever attempt to raise the veil except when he vaguely alludes to 'his people in the north;' but whether he means the north of England or the north of Scotland or the north of London none of us whom he honours with his acquaintance have ever been able to discover. If I might venture upon a suggestion, I fancy he knows more about the people of the east than of the north, from the nature of the monetary transactions he occasionally indulges in. Yet Davie, in spite of the secrecy with which he envelops his social surroundings, is quite a representative man of his order at the Caravanserai. At a glance you can tell to what calling he belongs. To the observing mind nothing is simpler than to identify a man with his profession. A hundred tricks of gait, attire, and talk reveal the soldier and the sailor. Without his white tie and black garb the parson, disguise himself as he may, is soon discovered. You can tell a barrister by the way he trims his whiskers, pulls about his nose, and rises and sits down. What tutored eye ever fails to recognise the solicitor, the doctor, the clerk, and the City man? All have peculiar movements and expressions inseparable from their walk in life, and which stamp them with the trade-mark of their calling. And who could ever make a mistake about Davie Benson? In his bell-shaped hat, so glossy and so curly; in the

small keen whiskerless face; in the tie, sporting yet not loud; in the frock-coat, fitting like a glove to his thin supple figure; in the tight trousers, the gait, and the gaiters and varnished boots, you read as plainly as if it were labelled on his back, Horseflesh. No one who does not spend much of his time in the saddle could walk in that peculiar style, and no one save he whose figure is always in strict training could be so emaciated and yet so powerful.

Standing little above five feet six, with not an ounce of superfluous flesh upon him, apparently as slight as a girl, there are not many who can surpass Davie in those feats which require both strength and dexterity for their accomplishment. The raking chestnut which carries him so well amid the pastures of Leicestershire, and which is the admiration of the grooms at the 'George,' knows the utter futility of attempting to free herself when in one of her moods from the iron hands that never move from her withers. The favourite pupil of Alick Reed, there are few more awkward customers to encounter at a bout with the gloves than Davie—who quicker than he at out-fighting or more clever in avoiding a rally? To watch him 'on the bench' handling an unruly team is a study of strength, tact, and patience; how soon the restive wheelers and the recalcitrant leaders find out that obstinacy is a mistake, and put an end to their opposition by stepping as well together as if they had been accustomed to leave Piccadilly every morning at ten and trot back in the evening at seven. Watch Davie turn in to scale after a three-mile match, '10st. 7lb. each, owners up,' over a stiffish hunting country: he is as cool and calm as if he had just come out of his morning tub, whilst his opponent is breathing like a walrus and streaming like a waterfall. Many a broad-shouldered powerful Goliath has had to acknowledge himself beaten by the endurance of this effeminate-looking David on the moors of Scotland, amid the streams of Norway and Canada, on the track of the big game, and wherever sport and pluck cater for disciples.

'It is all a question of condition,' says Davie quietly; 'the only difference between me and other men is that I am *always* in condition, whilst other men only occasionally are. A man says he will ride against me or run me for a mile or row against me from Putney to Mortlake, and forthwith he goes into severe training, but the moment the match is over drops back to his old life: dines late, takes brandies-and-sodas, eats too much, sleeps too much, drinks too much, everything too much, and substitutes mooning for exercise. It is not the training that does a man harm; it is the life he leads *after* the training, the sudden revulsion from a systematic asceticism to unbridled luxury. I am always in training, and my weight does not fluctuate a pound in a twelve-month. It is true I sit up late—except when I am going to ride or men have made some match or other for me—but as I never smoke and seldom drink it affects me less than it otherwise might. Besides, a man who is always taking severe exercise does not require much sleep. It is your idle, well-fed, luxurious man about town who is always ready for slumber. The prize pig cannot keep awake; a few hours' sleep is ample for the racehorse.'

He has need for this asceticism. What wealth, rank, and education are to other men, coolness, temperance, and endurance are to Davie. His physical qualities are his stock-in-trade, and should his nerve fail or he damage himself permanently steeplechasing, he would, metaphorically, have to put the shutters up and take the benefit of the act. Though he insures heavily in the 'Accidental,' the sum he would receive in case of mutilation or incapacity would, I fear, be but a poor compensation for the loss of income he would sustain. What Davie's income is it is difficult to ascertain, but it must be considerable. A man cannot lead the life he does, ride the horses he does, play the points he does, know the men he does, or undertake the financial operations he does, without having at his disposal a large amount of ready money. How does he amass it? If you study his career the reply is not difficult to find.

In these days of fierce competition, when every calling is crowded with pushing, eager, greedy followers, every man who comes to the front has something of great merit in him. He may not have all the brilliant qualities his friends allege, but assuredly he is not the mediocrity his enemies declare. In his own peculiar vocation Davie is a prominent man, and consequently a successful one. My acquaintance with him is slight, but whenever we meet he is always agreeable, and I am under obligations to him for picking me up, for a mere song, the handsomest roan cob that was ever trotted out at the Ranelagh. Nor do I fail to confess that there is much in Davie which calls forth my admiration. I respect his skill, his courage, his manly tastes and the splendid self-control he always exhibits. I have never seen him lose his temper, and I have heard less against his honour—honour nowadays being confined to the fulfilment of all pecuniary obligations—than one would expect from the peculiar life he leads. If he rides it is generally safe to back his mount; and if he does not rigidly eschew all the frauds of the turf, he has never acted in such a way as to draw upon himself censure, or to justify the desertion of his supporters. When he puts down his name, either at home or abroad, as one of the competitors at a dove tournament, he *means* to kill his bird, and it is through no fault or conspiracy of his if the blue-rock flies over the enclosure. His debts of honour are always scrupulously paid. When you make a bet with him he does not pretend to do you a favour, and then give you a point below the current odds. You may safely play *écarté* with him so far as scoring the king is concerned, though it is only fair to tell you that there are few men at the

'Méditerranée' at Nice who better know the game. If he sells you a horse he will certainly make his profit on the transaction, but the probability is that you will get a better and a cheaper animal than from the dealers. In short Davie knows the world so well as to be fully

alive to the advantages to be gained by having the reputation of a fair character. Honesty is not only morally the best policy, but also pecuniarily.

The social position that Davie occupies is, as I have said, a mystery to those of his acquaintance. He never speaks of his relations or of his early days, and that in itself is a secrecy somewhat open to suspicion. Men as a rule, after a certain amount of acquaintance, have no objection to let their fellows know to whom they belong, where they have been educated, and what county is their home; it is only the adventurer who is silent on such subjects. To repeat the rumours as to Davie's origin which gossip and calumny indulge in is idle. According to some, the bar sinister lies across his escutcheon; according to others, his parentage is legitimate, but his father was a convict, an unfrocked priest, a hatter, a horse-coper, a bankrupt warehouseman, a barrister, an undertaker, a soldier, a sailor, a tinker, a tailor; all which simply proves that my friend knows how to keep his own counsel; and that the world, as it always does when it is in utter ignorance about anything, substitutes imagination for information. Whatever may be Davie's antecedents, his social sponsor is Sir Rankesborough Gorse, the well-known sportsman and pillar of the turf. Where Sir Rankesborough met Davie and how an alliance between the two sprang up are questions which the inquisitive have not yet solved. Certain it is that Davie is the managing man of Sir Rankesborough's stud and controls all its arrangements, from the purchase of the yearlings to the dismissal of the trainer. He executes all Sir Rankesborough's racing-commissions, rides when required, and his opinion is law in the stable. More than once has his judgment been confirmed against an adverse majority; and in spite of the objections of the trainer and the fears of his patron, more than once has he selected some despised and overlooked animal which has carried the 'black and silver' colours of the baronet to victory. Can we not remember the hostility of the ring against Whitesocks, and how severe were the comments of the learned in horseflesh upon his somewhat abject appearance? yet Davie never once faltered in his decision, and, as we all know, the horse won 'the Guineas' in the commonest of canters. A knowledge of the noble animal is a great gift, and Davie ranks second to none in the possession of that information. Dealers know better than to palm off any of their dodges upon 'Sir Rankesborough's man'—their flattery, their doctoring, and all their cunning never deceive the keen cold eye that takes in at a glance both the character of the vendor and the points of the animal. I will back Davie to pick up a horse cheaper and sell it at a better profit than any man in England, whilst seldom incurring after reproaches from the purchaser.

The intimacy between Sir Rankesborough Gorse and David Benson is one of those friendships which benefits both the contracting parties. Since Davie has had the control of the baronet's stable the 'black and silver' has had no cause to complain; race after race has fallen to Sir Rankesborough's colours, till his lot have become the idols of the public. He has not yet won a Derby, but there is a certain yearling, bought by Davie at Marden Park some months ago, which will, I am sure, astonish the beholders when he makes his appearance on the Downs. To win a Derby is the one soul-absorbing ambition of Sir Rankesborough—an ambition which, unless I grievously mistake, will be gratified when the time arrives for that yearling aforesaid to strip in the paddock. On the other hand, 'the f'la that Sir Rankesborough picked up' has been admitted into a social atmosphere which, under less happy circumstances, he would not have breathed. It is through Sir Rankesborough that Davie has been elected a member of the Caravanserai and of the Verdure; it is through his connection with Sir Rankesborough that he gathers together the select specimens of *la jeunesse dorée* of our capital that are so often to be met with at his hospitable dining-table at Long's Hotel; it is to Sir Rankesborough that he owns his introduction to the messes of most of the crack regiments in the kingdom; in short, without the baronet, Davie would have remained a little stagnant puddle, isolated and alone, and hopelessly cut off from ever mingling with the brilliant stream of life.

Yet Davie, large as is his acquaintance, is essentially a man's man. Walk with him in the Park, and it is astonishing the number of friendly greetings that he has to acknowledge; but he has seldom an occasion to remove his hat, for rarely does a bonnet bow to him in graceful salutation. Men ask him freely to dinner at their clubs, but never dream of taking him home and introducing him to their wives and sisters. You meet him at bachelors' boxes, not at country houses. Whenever Davie talks about ladies he calls them 'modest women'—which the spiteful say shows that he knows very little of society. Intimate as he is with Sir Rankesborough, he no more knows Lady Mildred Gorse than does her ladyship's house-steward or head-groom. Nor does Davie object to this exclusion. Whether the society of ladies would bore him, or he is conscious of his social shortcomings, or whatever be the reason, he never seems hurt that his most intimate acquaintance keeps the women of his household from him, nor does he ever attempt to push his way into drawing-room or boudoir. He is quite content with his position in life and the manner he has played his cards, and he no more regrets that the doors of society are shut upon him than does a ring-man at Ascot that he is not admitted into the royal enclosure. Not that Davie is in any way objectionable, for, on the contrary, he is far more modest and presentable than many of his betters who have the *entrée* of the best houses in the town. If he is not 'a gentleman' he is an excellent imitation of the article; and if in manners, dress, and appearance somewhat horsey, in tone of honour and in sense of self-respect he is often the superior of those who sneer at him as 'the fellah Sir Rankesborough picked up.' The position occupied by Davie is, however, not an exceptional one. There are many men in London who, from their talents, their skill, their amusing qualities, their special knowledge of special subjects, live on the surface of society, comfortably, perhaps brilliantly, yet, by some tacit understanding between them and those they come in contact with, they never seek to penetrate deeper. A frontier line is drawn, and it must not be overstepped. The club, the suite of chambers, the hunting-box, the shooting-box, the moor, the deer-forest, the yacht, as much as you please; but the drawing-room requires credentials which it is not given to every one to possess. That passport is not among Davie's papers.

However uncertain and nondescript may be the

social position of Davie, there can be no question as to the certainty and substantiality of his income. In these days, when the professions are thronged, and commerce is venturesome, save to the large capitalist, a man might do worse, so far as money is concerned, than follow in the steps of Davie. The occupation of the *viveur* upon his wits is, however, not the simple matter it may appear to the ignorant. As the barrister has to study law, as the doctor has to walk the hospitals, as the merchant has to learn the duties of a clerk, and as the tradesman begins by being an apprentice, so men like Davie have to acquire their part and perfect themselves by severe application. That consummate skill in all their accomplishments, that steadiness of nerve, that coolness of head which neither the excitement of success intoxicates nor the mortification of failure irritates, that power of enduring fatigue, that pluck and strength, are not obtained without continual practice and the severest application. Watch Davie at Sandown or Croydon, at Liverpool or Warwick: with what judgment he rides, what patience he has, how well he knows when to force the running and when to wait upon his horses, and how exactly at the right time does he make his effort and scores another victory for the black and silver! Have that skill and judgment been obtained by aught than the severest labour? Mark Davie at the Gun Club, at

Baden, at Monaco, at Deauville, when he has backed himself to win a heavy sweepstake, or is pitted in a match against a formidable dove-slayer—the roar of the ring never disturbs him, the hopes of his admirers never fluster him, the consciousness of the fact that success may mean a fortune and defeat a heavy loss never ruffles his equanimity; he takes his breech-loader calmly from the man, surveys the brazen-throated book-makers with a smile, makes a few additional bets, perhaps, as he takes up his position, then, 'Are you ready?' 'Pull!' covers his bird, and the day must be very bad, or the blue-rock wonderfully wild, if it does not fall a victim on the sward. How many hours must he have spent before he educated his eye to attain that unerring aim! Again, watch Davie at billiards: how softly he plays his 'cannons' and makes his 'hazards,' whilst always managing to leave nothing on the table for his opponent! At pool, too, who more dead at taking 'lives,' or who more clever in nestling himself under the cushion, than he? But it is perhaps at whist that his peculiar gifts are the most dazzling. He has all the qualities necessary for a whist-player of the very first class—a splendid memory, a perfect temper, a clear head never clouded by the fumes of wine or tobacco (Oh, those after-dinner rubbers!), great powers of combination and concentration, and a lightning quickness for drawing inferences. He plays high—the loss of a 'bumper' at the Verdure is no joke—and when as confident in his partner as he is in his own genius, he does not scruple to back himself to a considerable extent. Yet his self-control never deserts him. Your true-born

Englishman, as a rule, when he is winning stops and pockets his gains, whilst he will back his ill-fortune to any extent, and plunge deeper and deeper, in the hopes of regaining his losses.

Davie is wiser in his generation. When in luck he

soon rushes his opponents into money. 'The great art of gambling,' he says, 'is to avoid losing your own coin, and to play boldly when Fortune favours you with your gains.' This theory he carries into practice. When he loses four rubbers running or five games of *écarté* straight off he withdraws from the table. 'I wish whist,' he remarks, 'to last me all my life; and if you lose four rubbers running, luck is against you, and you may, if you continue, lose another ten. No matter what are the points, to take up bad hand after bad hand interferes with your play and robs you of the pleasure of the game.' Like most men who gamble, Davie is a believer in *luck*; and, however much one may be unable logically to demonstrate that there is such a thing, there can be no question as to the fact of its existence. Any one who plays cards must have noticed how often Fortune clings to one man or to certain seats during an evening, whilst ill-luck of the most persistent description marks another man or the opposite seat for its own. Why? How? Who can tell? Watch the lucky man: what honours he holds, what cards he has, and how well he is always supported by his partner! The unlucky man, on the other hand, cannot escape from his temporary bad fortune; he may call for fresh cards, he may change his seat, he may adjure the fickle goddess by all the strangest forms of propitiation, yet the spell cannot be broken.

Since I have heard Davie's remarks, how often have I noticed that a man who loses four rubbers running continues to lose, and how often have five adverse games at *écarté* developed into ten and more! In all speculations nothing is certain; but as luck is on the whole even in its operations, he who is a good whist-player, and who declines to follow a run of misfortune, cannot fail to rise up a winner at the end of the year. Hence to Davie whist alone must be a comfortable annuity.

The young men at the Caravanserai to whom Davie is somewhat of an idol often speculate as to the sums he makes in a year. That he amasses wealth cannot be doubted. He is one of those men who whatever they touch turns into coin. What arrangements Sir Rankesborough enters into with him we know not; but Davie must draw a handsome share of the profits of the stable in addition to the sums he independently backs himself for when confident of his mount. From billiards and pool alone he must derive the income of a county court judge. Whist yields him large profits, which are considerably increased by his operations of systematically laying 'five to two' on the winners of the first game. 'I began,' he openly admits, in reference to these operations, 'with a capital of one thousand pounds—my capital, though it has had to bear some smartish fluctuations, is always intact at the end of the year, whilst my profits quite satisfy my modest requirements. To any man in search of a livelihood, I recommend the profession of laying five to two. The odds are always eagerly taken and seldom landed. Let a man begin with a capital of one hundred pounds, let him make himself acquainted with the respective merits of the players he is to back, and then let him systematically lay five pounds to two—using of course his judgment when to decline—and he will preserve his capital untouched, and make without difficulty three hundred a year.' Davie lays fifty to twenty, therefore the profits he derives from his proceedings can easily be ascertained by a simple sum of rule of three. Having an extensive acquaintance with men, the 'books' he makes on all the large races must allow him after every meeting to place a handsome sum at his bankers'.

Of late dark gentlemen with almond eyes, beaky noses, curly locks, and moist yellow complexions have been seen coming out of Davie's chambers, and I hear that my active young friend has recently taken to utilise his capital by indulging in certain very profitable speculations in land. Thus what with riding, betting, horse-coping, cards, billiards, pigeon-shooting, and backing himself generally for anything that he is likely to win, Davie must turn over annually a very handsome income. Knowledge is power, and the possession of wits is wealth. I do not say that the career is a perfectly reputable one—yet Davie has never been guilty of anything glaringly disreputable—still it has the advantage of being open to all who are endowed with the requisite physical and intellectual gifts. You do not require education, for from the mistakes in orthography that Davie makes in his letters asking you to dinner, and from the peculiar pronunciation of certain words, he can scarcely be called an educated man. You do not require good birth, or even good manners, or even capital to enter upon this somewhat outside profession. Still, though you may dispense with the learning from books, you must possess qualities which are, perhaps, after all rarer to find than the attainments of the scholar, before you can hope to make such a livelihood as falls to the lot of Davie Benson, Esq., of the north.

THE OLD SCHOOL.

THE OLD SCHOOL.

There are few things more distressing to a reflective mind than the attitude which the Church of England has assumed within the last generation. Disguise the matter as much as we may, there can be no doubt of the fact that the Anglican Church is fast becoming a Romish institution. In spite of the bench of bishops, the Thirty-nine Articles, and the decisions of the courts of law, many of our clergy preach to their congregations the creed pure and simple of the Roman Catholic Church. Enter many of our places of worship in London and in our country towns, and, unless told to the contrary, we might imagine that we were under the sway of the Vatican. The altar is gorgeously draped and lighted; incense renders the air heavy and sickly; the consecrated elements are held aloft for adoration; confession is openly taught from the pulpit and practised in the aisles; the clergy, not content with the title of priest, insist upon the designation of 'father;' banners with strange devices hang against the walls; and forms and ceremonies unknown to the Establishment are freely introduced into the services.

Between Ritualism on the one hand and Research on the other, it seems to me that the dear old Church of England of my youth must fall to the ground. It was once the pride of Englishmen to regard the creed they professed as the best and purest of all religions. It was manly without being destructive; it was Catholic without mummery; it was warmly attached to the State, and its teachers were gentlemen. Can the same now be said of the Church of England? In one parish we see a clergyman ashamed of his garb and his title; dressing like a layman and dropping the reverend; criticising the Bible as he would any ordinary historical work, and dismissing many of what have been considered the great truths of Christianity as unworthy of acceptance by any rational mind. Whilst in another parish we see its vicar acting more like an Italian than an Englishman, and doing his utmost to put down the Protestantism of the Church which he has solemnly sworn to support, and to erect in its place the faith of the Papacy. I decline to split hairs. I know that our Ritualists maintain they are not Papists; but when I see them inculcating the teaching of Rome, issuing little books of devotion coolly plagiarised from those of Rome, and imitating in their ceremonies, their attire, and their institutions the practices of Rome, it seems to me perfectly justifiable to say that they are Italian, and not English, Churchmen.

And it is from the Ritualists that we have the most to fear. The Broad Churchman appeals to the few

whose intellect is stronger than their faith; but the Ritualist appeals to that immense class, idle, weak, emotional, in whom the superstitious element is stronger than the intellectual. No one who has watched, even most superficially, the currents of society but must have perceived how they set, especially among the higher, or, to speak more correctly, the wealthier classes, towards Ritualism. We are living under a plutocracy, and Ritualism is essentially the religion for the rich. In Ritualism plutocracy sees itself reflected: it is the caricature of an ancient faith, as the plutocrat is himself the caricature of the aristocrat; it is gay and gaudy, and fond of pomp and show like the plutocrat; it is arrogant and self-asserting, its priests concealing their want of birth and scholarship by the robes of sacerdotal pretensions, as the plutocrat himself attempts to hide his deficiencies by the display of his wealth and money power; it is shallow, unscrupulous, and miserably effeminate. Yet no sensible man can attempt to deny that Ritualism is now an immense force in the country, and one that is daily extending its power.

A society that is rich, that is idle, that has little to occupy its leisure, must betake itself to some form of distraction. Men have their professions and their ambition to engage their minds; but it is upon the women that idleness falls as a rule with so heavy a hand. Balls, dinners, and intrigue that is politely called flirtation will occupy the leisure of many; still there are others to whom social dissipation is a routine of boredom, and who seek after a more refined excitement. If they have a taste for art, science, or literature, they are fortunate;

but these are the exceptions, not the rule. And now it is that that strange creation of the nineteenth century, the Anglican priest, steps in and opens out a path for work and action. The young woman whose matrimonial chances are not yet decided, the disappointed middle-aged woman, the elderly dame with no domestic cares, all find their allotted labour—a round of ceremonial observances and duties occupy all their leisure. The nineteenth-century dame, be she spinster, childless wife, or widow, need have no cause to mourn over the leaden wings of Time. The Ritualist comes to her aid, and *ennui* and inactivity are no more. What with attending early celebrations, matins, confession, vespers, and midnight services; attaching herself to a sisterhood; visiting a certain class of sick and poor under strict clerical supervision; interesting herself in church decorations, pestering her friends for endless contributions, and distributing little sentimental works of devotion, the day is, in fact, too short for her—so short, indeed, that she is often unable to assist her mother in the concerns of her household, or to add by her presence to the geniality of the domestic circle.

We are so wealthy that we wish our religion, like our houses and other appointments, to be in keeping. The robes of our clergy must be splendid; and our clergy, who are now for the most part literates instead of graduates, have no objection that the cope should hide the want of the university hood; our churches must be ornate and artistic; we must have music, flowers, banners, elaborate altar-cloths, and everything that fascinates the eye and inspires the senses. The old-fashioned faith of our fathers has gone to its rest, and save in some obscure village, where people go to worship and not to perform, is hard to be met with. Sentimental pietism is now religion; an adherence to a host of silly ceremonial observances stands in the place of duty; and faith is now only another word for a belief in the 'priest.' It is idle to talk to Englishmen of the devotion of the Anglican priest, the purity of the Anglican nun, and the zeal of the Anglican monk now working within our midst. Innovators are always zealous and devoted till their system is established. But we have had the system before; and we know, three hundred years ago, what the priesthood, the nunnery, and the monastic order resulted in. History is apt to repeat itself; we have no wish to see those scenes repeated.

There is one dear friend of mine who cordially sympathises with these views, whom it is always a great pleasure to see at the Caravanserai. Hubert Marborough is a type of the old English clergyman which is, unhappily for us, fast dying out. A man of unfeigned piety, an active yet not fussily inquisitive rector, a good classic, and a most perfect gentleman in all his tastes and feelings, he is the last of that class which Sydney Smith called the 'squarsons.' A second son, he was destined for holy orders, and was duly installed in the family living of Hettiscombe. Ten years after having taken his ordination vows, his elder brother was drowned with his only son whilst yachting in the Mediterranean, and Hubert suddenly found himself transformed from a country parson, with a living of eight hundred a year, into a squire with a rent-roll of some annual twelve thousand. Many men under these circumstances would have quitted the Church, and have forgotten the priest in the country gentleman. Not so Hubert Marborough. He exchanged the rectory for the old hall, letting his curates dwell in the house that he had deserted; but he still worked his parish, visited his poor, and preached his sermons as became a man who had put his hand to the plough and declined to look back.

The only difference that fortune made in him was to extend immensely his powers for doing good. He pays his curates well, neither patronising them nor despising them, but treating them like gentlemen, though he is very particular as to their belonging either to the one or the other of our two Universities, and to their style of reading. He can forgive a young clergyman a good many things, but he will *not* forgive him for dropping his *h*'s or making a false quantity. He has established a dispensary and a good useful library, in which humorous works are not excluded, in the village. He sees that every cottage on his estate is put into repair, and

made not only habitable but comfortable. One of the sternest of magistrates on the bench to the tramp and the vagrant, his hand is ever ready to alleviate misery and suffering. Nor does he perform his acts of charity by deputy, for none knows better than he how a kind word and a friendly greeting enhance a gift from the rich to the poor. It is his hand that often tucks the warm clean blankets around the bed of the rheumatic peasant, or administers the nourishing soup or the dry old port to the weak and the sickly. It is his smile and chat that are almost as welcome to the honest man temporarily out of work as is the little present of ready money. The poor dame, who has just become a mother, knows well enough to whom to apply, if she is ordered by the village doctor what it is impossible for her husband to supply her with. Though an opulent squire, the chairman of quarter sessions, and allied by marriage to a powerful earl in his county, none of the poor stand in awe of him. If they want advice or assistance they scruple less to go to him than to one of the curates. Yet, gentle and loving as is their pastor, they know better than to try to use any of the wiles of the suppliant. In spite of his large heart and intense amiability, Hubert Marborough has a keen eye for character, and can be as repellent as the harshest if he suspect imposition. He is the tenderest of shepherds to his flock, but he is quite up to all the gambols of the black sheep.

Of all the broad counties in England I know no fairer than that of—let me call it—Quartzshire. For the combination of mountain and moor, wood and water, it stands unrivalled. To the artist with his æsthetic eye, its hilly passes, richly-clothed valleys, thickly-timbered forests, and picturesque varieties which the landscape is ever unfolding, are as full of charm as are the well-stocked trout-streams and the wild moorland, broken by hill and dale, to the sportsman. In one of its most lovely spots, watered by the broad current of—let me say—the Mica, and within gunshot of the spledid Knole Wood, stands Hettiscombe, a large white building with columns and porticoes, on the brow of one of the numerous undulations that surround the neighbourhood. A fine park, severed in twain by a lake fed by the river Mica, encircles the house, whilst in the rear is the wood, with its tall waving firs and mysteries of shade. Away in the distance the great upland region of Sleignmoor can be seen, with all its variety of hill and valley, bog and stream; whilst, like Cyclopean castles, the gigantic masses of weathered granite rise at intervals to crown the famous Tors.

Approaching the house, one sees from the balconied terraces and well-kept lawn and gardens that the place is carefully looked after; yet it is not merely as a country seat that Hettiscombe is dear to me. No doubt, amid the stately mansions of this old England of ours, there is many a castle and hall which, so far as architecture, luxury, and appointments are concerned, is the superior of Hettiscombe; but where shall I find such a *home?* Running down from London, with its cynical tone, its artificial pleasures, and its wearying round of excitement, to Quartzshire, no sooner have you passed a couple of days with the family of Hubert Marborough than you look upon life very differently from what you have been accustomed to do in Pall Mall. Perhaps, for the first time, it strikes you that there is something higher than mere pleasure, something nobler than selfishness, something truer and more comforting than mundane philosophy. The manner in which a man brings up his family has always been to me the best test of his character and of the strength of his principles, and I know no more charming sight than the home-life of Hettiscombe. The daughters are simple, well-bred, and unaffected; the sons are free from the slang of the barrack and the stable; whilst between parents and children, and husband and wife, there is that exquisite harmony of feeling caused by affection, self-respect, and a clear conscience.

A spirit of the most fascinating cheerfulness pervades the whole establishment, and even finds itself reflected amongst the stable-helps, a notoriously discontented class. The old vicar talks to his wife as if the honeymoon had never dissolved itself into the silver wedding, and the sisters only wrangle amongst themselves in trying to spoil their brothers when on leave from their regiments, or at home during 'the Long.' Though the house is seldom free from visitors, yet there is no need for the presence of the stranger to give a fillip to the often monotonous round of domesticity. The vicar is quite happy among his books and papers, thinning his

trees, cantering about the moorland on his old white hunter, or making a round of calls in the parish. Lady Mary, it seems to me, is never so content as when, in big hat and gauntlet gloves, she is pottering about the garden, whilst her husband, in the roomiest of Indian chairs, is seated within call, studying the advertisements in the *Field*, or reading the clerical speeches in the *Guardian*. The girls amuse themselves in a thousand ways with a sense of consideration for each other's tastes and wishes not always to be observed amongst sisters; whilst the brothers seem so proud of the successes of each other—Hal has got the good-conduct sword at Woolwich, Dick has won the cup as best shot at Hythe, Reggie has been complimented by the judge for the way in which he conducted his case—as utterly to preclude all feelings of secret jealousy. When the visitor arrives he is made not only welcome, but feels, no matter how shy by nature, completely at home. Without any fuss or obtrusive activity, he finds the whole family consulting his wishes, laying before him proposals exactly in accordance with his tastes, leaving him alone when he desires, or giving him plenty of society when solitude is unacceptable.

And one of the charms of Hettiscombe is, that you never meet disagreeable people. However cantankerous a man's or woman's nature is, I do not believe he or she could be long in that irritable state under the influence of the cheery piety of the rector, and of the sunny presence of his household. The most suspicious cannot but feel, however much they may differ from him, that Hubert Marborough is a good and single-minded man.

Listen to his conversation, watch him as narrowly as you please in all the relations of life, hear him pray and preach, observe the example he sets his family, and you cannot come to any other conclusion than that you are in the society of one who, without a doubt or reservation, believes in the doctrine he professes, and essays to carry out all that it teaches. A Low Churchman of the old school, he is as devoid of the intolerance and acidity of certain of his brethren as he is of the mummery and sickly sentimentalities of the Ritualist. He is an Englishman, with the healthy tastes and aspirations of an Englishman. Old as he is there are few men in his part of the county, did he think hunting a sport that became his profession, who are better riders to hounds; and in spite of his waning sight I would sooner back the rector's breechloader to bring down more birds, either in the coverts or on the moors, than that of many a younger man who fancies 'himself.'

Marborough can get on with most people, and long as I have known him never have I heard him utter a spiteful remark or give heed to scandal. Frivolous and malicious gossip he abominates, and its entire absence from the conversation of the household of Hettiscombe is one of the peculiarities of that charming home. Never do you hear any of the slander about the lord-lieutenant, the bishop, or the neighbouring clergy and gentry, which forms so large a part of the conversation of the country. The rector's maxim is that of good old Archbishop Tillotson, if you can say no good of a man, at least say no evil. Yet there is one class of people he cannot agree with. He sternly refuses to countenance the Ritualists. He can understand, and to a certain extent sympathise with, a man who is a Roman Catholic or a Dissenter or a Jew or even a Freethinker, but he can neither understand nor sympathise with one whom he regards as a traitor to the Church of England. To his keen sense of honour it seems inconceivable that a man should continue to draw his stipend from the Church whose teaching he declines to accept and whose discipline he seeks to subvert. It is open to any one who differs from the creed of the Church of England to go outside her pale; but, in the opinion of Marborough, it is mean and dishonest in the extreme to receive the pay of the Church and to wear her uniform whilst working for the enemy. In vain the Ritualists around Hettiscombe have sought to convert Hubert Marborough to their way of thinking. His church is sound, solid, air-tight, water-tight, warm, and comfortable; he will not have it 'restored.' Vestments have no charms for him; when he reads prayers he wears his surplice and university hood, and when he preaches he appears in the pulpit in a black gown. He does not believe in incessant church services and in constant celebrations of the Holy Communion, for in his eyes these only fatigue the clergy and make worship mechanical. But he believes in helping the sick and needy, in visiting the widow in her affliction, and in succouring the distressed. When spoken to of the advantages of the system of confession, he mildly replies that he 'has travelled in Italy, France, and Spain, and he has yet to learn that the morality in those countries is superior to that in England.'

During the month of May, when the meetings at Exeter Hall and St. James's Hall are held, my host of Hettiscombe always turns up at the Caravanserai. His figure is quite one of the curiosities of the club. There is no mistaking that tall slender form, now somewhat bowed with age, that high broad-brimmed hat with the healthy smiling face beneath, that frill jutting out of the black sporting-looking waistcoat, till it loses itself within the folds of the capacious white neckcloth; no mistaking that loose untidy-looking black coat, with the side-pockets wide open, suggestive of samples; those wonderful trousers, tight below the knee, yet voluminous enough in all conscience above; those rough cloth gaiters; those thick serviceable shoes! Thus attired, the rector-squire looks the very opposite of many of his clerical brethren, with their smug suits of shiny black and their atrocious head-gear—a hideous compromise between a billycock and the hat of a cardinal.

There are many married men to whom a run up to London and a fortnight at the club are the most delightful of changes. Not so with Hubert Marborough. As he wanders about the rooms of the Caravanserai, taking up one newspaper after the other, fidgeting about from chair to chair, you can see at a glance that he is not at home. At breakfast the little table, with its bachelor equipments, is a poor substitute for the long broad board at Hettiscombe, with its snow-white cloth and graceful medley of fruit and flowers amid the toast and scones and rolls and the old-fashioned silver dishes. He misses, like most men blessed with many children, the talk and society of the family circle; and he says his tea never tastes the same unless poured out by his eldest daughter. When he surveys the daily bill of fare, swinging on its frame, he looks at it helplessly, undecidedly, and is grateful to the butler when he suggests what should be ordered for dinner. He agrees with the Apostle, that a little wine for the stomach's sake is a good thing; and he also agrees with the Apostle that it should be *wine*, and not logwood juice, or some other vile decoction calculated to give the drinker acute heartburn within twenty minutes. At Hettiscombe he knows he can rely upon the contents of his cellar-book; but the club wine-list is a publication with which he is not so familiar; the names of many of the wine-merchants are new to him; several of the clarets are unknown to him; and as he sips his port-wine after dinner (our ports are *not* famous at the Caravanserai) I fancy he sighs after the vintages he is accustomed to

at home. He declines to take a house in town for the season, because he is unwilling to quit his parish for any length of time; and as his wife and daughters have no fancy to leave the country when it is most beautiful for the dust and heat of London, the rector generally spends his month *en garçon*. Occasionally his family come up; but after three weeks at Thomas's Hotel they pine for the shade and breezes of their west-country home, and take their departure.

As the club scarcely suits the domestic instincts of my friend, it is very fortunate that he has seldom occasion to find himself within its walls. As a representative Low Churchman, and one of the pillars of the National, Hubert Marborough is the welcome guest of the London evangelical world. He dines out at sedate mansions, where the festivities of the evening conclude with an exposition of Scripture and family prayers. At evangelical Drawing-rooms, assembled to encourage missionary or philanthropic enterprise, he often takes the chair, and offers a handsome contribution to the institution pleaded for when the velvet bag or china plate makes its begging round. He is always one of the speakers at the anniversaries of the great Low Church societies, and has frequently been asked to preach their annual sermon. He is on the committee of most of the religious institutions of his party, and is the president of one or two little benevolent 'homes' and 'refuges,' which he has founded, and which, if the truth were known, are mainly supported by his generosity. Young ladies who write anecdotes of the poor, or little stories with a moral, are always petitioning him to draw up a preface, or to allow them to introduce his name, so as to encourage the sale of their literary undertakings. For the rector-squire of Hettiscombe, apart from the sermons and addresses that he has published, is one of the most fertile of the polemical writers of his party. Not a movement is made by the Ritualists but he exposes the danger to be apprehended from their insidious proceedings. No sooner does a freethinking divine indulge in reflections contrary to the spirit and teaching of the Thirty-nine Articles than the rector of Hettiscombe boldly comes to the front, and does his best to refute them.

Thus Hubert Marborough, from his social position, his wealth, and his decided views, is looked up to as one of the leaders of his party. His advice is courted by his bishop, and young evangelical vicars and curates decline to form an opinion upon any great clerical question until they know the views of the divine of Hettiscombe. My friend no doubt has his faults, like all of us; but when his exquisite conscientiousness, his single-minded piety, his high tone of honour, his practice to the very letter of all that he preaches, are compared with the life and morality of the rest of the world, he seems to me one of the very few who really deserve that noblest title on the roll of Honour, that of—a Christian and a gentleman.

SOCIAL AMBITION.

SOCIAL AMBITION.

EVER since the days when Horace asked of Mæcenas how it came to pass that no one was satisfied with the position that the gods had placed him in, discontent has been the lot of humanity. What is a source of envy to one man is a source of disappointment to another. Here is a distinguished statesman, whose lofty wisdom has influenced the councils of Cabinets and guided the policy of the State; yet in his heart of hearts he would gladly sacrifice all his past reputation could he but gain a niche in the temple of fame as a great author. There is a gallant soldier, whose broad breast, covered with hardly-won decorations, bears witness to the brilliant services he has rendered his country; yet he is indifferent to the laurels won by his sword, and is only solicitous after those he is never likely to gain by his brush as an artist. A third sees the distance between himself and the woolsack lessening year after year; yet, careless of his name as a splendid lawyer, he aspires after the reputation of a Lovelace, and curses Nature, which has endowed him with brains, for neglecting to adorn his face. Were not Richelieu, Mazarin, Somers, Walpole, far prouder of their conquests in the boudoir than of their victories in the Senate? A fourth has raised himself to a leading position in the republic of letters; yet would he throw all his manuscripts to the wind to be considered a man of fashion. A fifth lends loans to empires, and by a word of acceptance or refusal can influence the markets of the world; yet all his wealth is powerless to buy what he covets with cravings that can never be satisfied—the blue blood of ancient lineage. Around us we see soldiers who would they were divines, divines who would they were statesmen, lawyers who wish to be artists, philosophers who wish to be men of fashion, peers who would they were demagogues, republicans who would sell their souls for a coronet—men of war, men of science, men of industry, men of idleness—all dissatisfied with their position in life, and longing after the unattainable. The question put to the illustrious descendant of Tuscan kings is as applicable now as then. 'How is it, Mæcenas,' asks the genial pagan, 'that no one lives content with his condition, whether Reason gave it him or Luck threw it in his way, but praises those who have different pursuits?'

Yet is this question only the echo of the cry of the bard-king who had drunk the chalice of life to the very dregs, and found the cup but vanity of vanities, all was vanity. In this best of all possible worlds no one is completely happy, no one is so thoroughly contented with his lot—however brilliant that lot may appear to the outsider—as not to hanker after what he has not. The barrister, up whose staircase solicitors never ascend, no doubt looks upon the illustrious occupier of the woolsack as the happiest and most fortunate of men; yet perhaps his lordship is a martyr to dyspepsia or the gout, or his wife makes his home-life unbearable, or his eldest son goes to the bad, or there hangs over his head some scandal of the past which he is ever in terror of being made public, or there is some other decoction of the *amari aliquid* which mars the completeness of his enjoyment. However well furnished our houses and ornate their appointments, there exists a skeleton in every cupboard; and not a tenant but fears, at some time or other, that either he or his guests will hear the rattling of its bones. Conscience makes cowards of us all. We know in what particular apartment of our mansion is suspended that attenuated spectre, and we dread lest it walk down-stairs and expose itself to our disgrace. Perhaps we give ourselves the airs of the choicest Lafitte or of '42 port; how, then, should we like the skeleton to visit our cellar and show us up as *vin ordinaire* of the thinnest of vintages? Or it may be that we pretend to be as wealthy as our neighbour;

how, then, should we approve of that lean monster quitting his retreat, and holding up our banker's book to the world, and revealing our miserable shifts and petty economies to make both ends meet? We say we are as brave as Agamemnon: should we care for the arm of the skeleton to strip the lion's skin from off our shoul-

ders, and expose us in our true asinine garb? We are religious, and looked up to by the neighbourhood; but have we no stories in the book of our life to which we would rather that that bony finger did not point? We are high born or well connected, and we pretend to intimate relations with certain in the *Peerage* or the

Landed Gentry; can it, then, be desirable for our cupboard tenant to be let loose, and to disclose those little flaws in our genealogical tree which somewhat rudely disturb the purity, or perhaps the legitimacy, of our descent? And so each one of us shuts up his peculiar skeleton, stows his bones effectively out of sight and smell, and tries to forget that so ghastly a visitor is in the family. But our precautions are in vain: close as we keep the secret of its prison, not a friend who calls upon us but is perfectly aware of the existence of our disagreeable lodger, and, blind to the fact that we know all about the anatomical remains in *his* closet, pities us accordingly. My good sir, if you wish to preserve anything from the public eye, expose it; conceal it, and it will be criticised, inquired into, and disclosed before you are many hours older.

My friend, little Freddy West, has a secret which he fancies he cleverly conceals from us of the Caravanserai. He, too, is under the impression that his skeleton is most safely locked up, and that none of his friends have ever heard its bones rattle. The son of a most respectable City tea-merchant (everybody in Mincing-lane knows the firm, Leaf, West, Grounds, & Co.), who has made a large fortune, I am given to understand, out of his dealings with the Chinese in opium, and with the English in bohea, Freddy declines to have any connection with the paternal warehouse. The little impostor scorns trade and all its belongings, and, thanks to manufactured crest and manipulated arms, lays claim to belong to a distinguished Kentish family. When asked by the stranger, in all innocence, whether he is related to the noble house whose armorial bearings he has assumed, he replies quietly, 'Yes, but we are the younger branch;' and drops the subject. In common with so many of his class, he 'double-barrels' his name. His mother, a Miss Farningham, the daughter of a small country vicar, he was christened Frederick Farningham; and consequently he has now blossomed forth as F. Farningham-West, leaving the uninitiated to imagine, by the adoption of the hyphen, that in his veins is not only the blood of the Wests, but that he will succeed to some of the family property. It has much amused me, when the waiter has written Freddy's name on a bit of paper, and placed it on the table which that young gentleman wishes to secure for dinner, to hear one of the enlightened of the club, on ascertaining who is to be his prandial neighbour, remark, 'O yes, he is one of the Delawarr lot, you know; his father, a younger son, married a Sackville West, had a pot of money with her, and took the name. That young fellow is the heir to a rattling good fortune.' Of such is the accuracy of the world.

Whatever may be the wealth of West *père*, very

little of its golden stream will flow into the pockets of the son. Educated at Harrow and afterwards at Oriel, Freddy, after having obtained his degree, declined to sit on a three-legged stool, to pore over ledgers or to look after customers. In an age which sees the sons of some of the first families in the country covet partnerships in good mercantile houses, young West, whose social instincts were strong, felt that he had a soul above commerce, and pined after a prominent position in what his father called 'the West-end.' As he added up the books, examined dock-warrants, or watched the expectorations of the tea-taster, visions of intimacies with men of fashion, of flirtations with high-born dames, of the portals of society opened *à deux battants* before him, revealing all the pleasures and hospitalities of a graceful and refined civilisation, conjured themselves up before his envious gaze. He wanted to be a 'swell' and to belong to the order. He had nothing in common with business and its surroundings. He hated the loud noisy men, who came into the office with their hats on the side of their heads, who slapped him vigorously on the back and wanted 'to know if the governor was in.' Careful and fastidious in his dress, he objected to run about the lanes and alleys of the City on mercantile errands, like a bank-clerk. The partners did not come up to his standard of what gentlemen should be; he declined to laugh at their stories whilst he corrected their grammar. His airs and graces so grievously offended many of the firm's best clients that they went away in anger and took their custom to a rival.

Nor did Freddy attend to the work intrusted to him. He came late and went away early. He read the newspapers instead of the letters. He preferred to lunch at the Caravanserai to the cookshops patronised by the other partners. He was far more eager to obtain invitations to dance or dinner than to beat up for customers. In short, he was worse than useless in the firm, and his father had no alternative but to turn him out. Freddy, intent upon exploring the realms of society, had long quitted the paternal villa at Dulwich, and between son and sire there was little love lost. Accordingly the young man found himself the possessor of the interest on 10,000*l.*, strictly tied up, and with not a hope of obtaining a farthing beyond. His second brother, who had been educated at a City school, and who was perfectly content with suburban life, was taken into partnership, and doubtless will one day develop into a merchant-prince.

Idle, independent, ambitious, Freddy strained all his efforts to get into good society. It was up-hill work, and he made little progress. A young man, against whom there is nothing notorious, has several ways at the present day of entering society, should his kith and kin be unable to command the ordinary mode of ingress. A good tenor voice will open the doors of houses which otherwise would be closed. A marked capacity for private theatricals is in itself an introduction to the highest. An amusing talker will generally end by finding his legs under the mahogany in most desirable dining-rooms. Music, comic songs, a talent for getting up cotillons, mimicry, ventriloquism, conjuring, are all means to an end. I know one man who was asked out a good deal simply and solely because he had a name as being a clever designer of monograms, in the days when monograms were the rage. Where he dined he had to design; as another man, where he dines, has to sing, play, amuse, or talk. Society conducts its hospitalities on a very commercial basis. You are welcome because you are noble, illustrious, famous, or wealthy, and thus by your presence reflect credit on your host and hostess. If you are none of these things, you are invited because you take the place of the professional singer, musician, or entertainer. There is no obligation on either side. You get your dinners out of society, and society gets its equivalent out of you. But to the man who has no equivalent to offer, society is the coldest of hosts. And this was the case with Freddy. He had enough to live on with economy, but nothing more. In spite of his sham pedigree the secret of his origin was known to all. He was not musical, he had no voice, he was a bad waltzer, he was not particularly amusing, he could not act, he had no special gifts likely to bear him on their tide to social success. Season after season passes, and he finds himself no nearer to the goal of his ambition than when he started.

Yet he employs all the devices of the unadmitted. He knows a good many men, but they do not take him to their houses. He hunted one winter at Melton, and he took a share in a yacht one summer at Cowes; but neither of these moves led to anything. He travels a good deal; but the English he knows abroad drop him when they cross the Channel. He has taken an active part in politics; but though the members whose elections he has been instrumental in obtaining gladly ask him to meet their constituents at a club-dinner, and seek his coöperation on platforms at meetings, these are not exactly the rewards he desires. He has essayed the religious line, in the hope that when in the one world he might scale the boundary-wall and find his way into the other. Yet in vain. He has interested himself in parish-work under the auspices of a fashionable London vicar; he has taught in schools; he has visited the poor; he has asked the curates to dinner; he has subscribed to causes he does not care about, and to missions he never before heard of: but all his energy and hypocrisy have been useless. He was invited to a *conversazione* and a drawing-room meeting or two, but he made no acquaintances. The vicar and the fashionable district-visitors were charmed to meet him on parochial matters, and to give him a long list of the poor he was to visit; but they did not consider that an interest in alleviating surrounding distress, however admirable and praiseworthy such feelings might be, necessarily led to social intimacy. 'That game is no go,' said Master Freddy to himself; 'damme, I don't want to know the poor—I want to know the rich.' To us who were somewhat behind the scenes this episode in our little friend's life was very amusing.

Thus it has happened that the aims Freddy set before him have never been realised. He is still, though on the verge of thirty, to use a favourite word of his, an 'outsider.' In his modest lodgings in Duke-street no invitations arrive of the nature he desires; no well-appointed carriage, with its fair well-dressed occupants, calls for him at the club to take him out for a drive; when he takes his walks abroad it is seldom that he has occasion to lift his hat and make his bow. He hovers between two social spheres, and belongs to neither. He is not of the great world, and he is not of the commercial world. Holding in horror trade, and clinging with such tenacity to the Farningham-West imposition that he ends by almost believing it, he has completely severed himself from his father's friends and relations. On the few occasions when he has put in an appearance at the parental table, he has become livid with suppressed rage at the boorish fashion in which his sire partakes of the dishes he loves, at the vulgar caps and colours his mother wears, at the English spoken by his brothers, and at the want of breeding of his sisters. It is not a happy gathering. The family look upon Freddy as 'a swell,' and stand in awe of him; whilst West *père*, hot with drink and sulky, glares at his first-born as if he would like, but dare not, to kick him into the road.

Yet in the whole realms of Pall Mall there is not a more miserable little creature than Freddy. Thanks to his tailor and hatter, a neat figure and an agreeable appearance, he looks like a gentleman; but in his views and sentiments he has little in common with the name. To rank he is prepared to pardon every shortcoming; and so long as men and women are born in the purple, he extenuates every fault and vice they commit. He worships birth and all the surroundings of fashion as only one of the middle class, who is ashamed of the order to which he belongs, can worship them. 'Blood' is to him all what religion is, all what principle is, all what honour, truth, morality are to other men. He does not respect rank as it is only right that it should in this country be respected, but he regards it with the most slavish adulation. If the son of a peer is a knave, or the daughter of a peer hideous, he will find the one honourable and the other a beauty. He detests every class but the one to which he does not belong, and into which he cannot gain admittance. He is indifferent to anything for its own sake; but if an undertaking be encouraged by the peerage, he likes to see his name amongst those who have given a guinea. He is the best of men to visit a fancy bazaar, for a duchess or a countess can wheedle him out of half of his monthly allowance. He seldom plays whist; but when he finds that any 'swells' are in the card-room of the Caravanserai, he will cut in and be proud to lose his money in such good company. On the slightest encouragement he will strike up an acquaintance with men of fashion, and economise for a fortnight to ask them to a dinner, which they never return. Though not in the world, he takes great pains to appear to be of it. He studies all the fashionable newspapers, and makes himself familiar with the movements of the leaders of society. He knows what receptions are to be held, and what balls and dinners are to be given, during the week. He has learnt his Burke almost by heart, and makes it his business to be familiar with the marriages that are to take place during the season. He knows by sight all the great people in town, and is a very useful man to escort country cousins to the Opera or the Park. Such people imagine him to be a buck of the first water, for he points out to them the beauties amongst the women and the distinguished amongst the men; and freely, when in their company, takes off his hat to carriages as they drive past, but whose occupants, a keen observer will notice, decline to return the salutation. He casually inquires of these rustics whether they are going to Lady

Dash's dance to-night, or to the Duchess of Blank's reception to-morrow; and when they modestly say, 'O dear no; we know no one in London!' he manages to convey the impression to their minds that he of course is amongst the invited.

As he is only happy in the society of those who, as it were, bolster up his social position, he is the most abject of toadies. If one of the few really great men who belong to the Caravanserai enters the club, Freddy will follow him about with his eyes, examine his dress, and watch how he eats, sits down, or reads the newspaper. When the young men of fashion, who belong to that world whose joys he so fiercely covets, hang about the hall in groups before driving out to the houses to which they are invited, he hovers near them and listens to their conversation. How he admires those 'swells,' who talk quite simply and naturally of the great people they know, nor seem to be much impressed by the favours accorded to them! I verily believe if Mephistopheles would come up and offer Freddy a peerage, and all the advantages attached to it, he would have no difficulty in coming to terms about my little friend's soul. Aware that he is not what he wishes to be and what he pretends to be (it is amusing how jealously he keeps the secret of his commercial origin, and how patent that secret is to all of us!), young West is utterly deficient in self-respect, and in the higher qualities of true manhood. In his heart he feels himself, to use a term of reproach he is rather fond of casting at others, a 'snob;' and as long as he holds the mean views of life he entertains, even were he the son of a duke, he richly deserves the name. Freddy *is* a snob. He has the tricks of imposition of the snob, the servile admiration of the snob, that mixture of deference for the great and contempt for the lowly only to be found in the snob, and he suffers the needless mental tortures of the snob.

When I see Freddy and listen to his conversation, I cannot help moralising on man's discontent. Here is a young fellow born to what many would envy. He entered upon life under most favourable auspices. For him the anxiety and struggle which fall to the lot of the man who has to make a career did not exist. The family business was already founded; he had only to follow in his father's footsteps to be a wealthy man. He had a home (it might, perhaps, be in better taste, but one cannot have everything) such as only money could furnish and keep up. His family doted upon him until his contemptible affectation alienated them from him. He could have had troops of friends to cheer and amuse him. He could have led a happy, manly, and contented life. He had nothing to be ashamed of. His father was an upright honest man, whose good name had never been tarnished by sharp practice or fraudulent proceedings. It was true that he was in trade; and pray, Master Freddy, who is not in trade in these days? The father may have just reason to be ashamed of the son, but certainly not the son of the sire.

Yet Freddy has sacrificed all these advantages for the emptiest of ambitions; he has lost everything and gained nothing. He is nobody. He never will have more than some eight hundred a year. He would like to marry, but he refuses to marry into his father's set, and he has little chance of marrying outside it. He has no friends but those who ridicule him for his failings.

His life is passed in sham, hypocrisy, and unhappiness. *Cui bono?* Even from his own point of view he has played his cards badly. Had he humoured his father and been diligent in business there was nothing to prevent him, good-looking and well-mannered, and with Fortune at his back, from working his way, as many have before him, into the society he so warmly admires. As a member of the great Plutocracy he would have had no occasion to go forth into the highways and byways to find 'friends;' nor, when once the extent of his means was ascertained, need he have despaired of making an excellent alliance. He had a future before him which might have been brilliant, but which certainly would have been comfortable. The future that now stares him in the face is a blank; for let Freddy wish as much as he may, the portals of the paternal firm are shut against him. Nor will it be long, from what I hear, before the doors of the Dulwich villa will follow the example of the warehouse in Mincing-lane. If ever man gave up the substance to grasp the shadow, it is F. Farningham-West; and there must be times, I fancy, when he and his skeleton pass many a *mauvais quart d'heure* together. I should not care to be present at those interviews.

BOHEMIA.

BOHEMIA.

It has been well said that the one half of the world does not know how the other half lives. We each of us move in our own sphere, follow its habits, accept its teaching, and adopt its customs. Of the vast world outside our own petty circle—of its struggles for existence, of its professional wiles, of its feuds, jealousies, and observances—we know no more than the Chinaman, who writes down all beyond his dominions as barbarians. As in geology each stratum has its separate and distinct formation, so in social life each class has its own peculiarities of manner, industry, and amusement, which reveal the order to which it belongs. What is permitted in the one class is not tolerated in the other; what is pleasure to the one would be regarded as the most irksome of restraints by the other. If there were no lines of demarcation separating the one class from the other, the very differences in the mode of life and in the ways of thought would prove in themselves obstacles sufficiently insurmountable to prevent fusion between such discordant elements.

Take the Bohemian as an example. To him the fetters of civilisation are insupportable; he declines to obey the commands of society and the code of morals it draws up. The homage to rank and wealth, the emptiness of general conversation, the monotony of routine, the attention paid to outward adornment, are all eminently distasteful to him. A man generally with some pretensions to art or literature, he infinitely prefers to chat with an artist over his pictures or with an author over his manuscripts than to add his name to the crowd of nobodies which throng the reception-rooms of a lady of fashion, or to take part in the feebleness and platitudes of ordinary social talk. Fond of the society of women, he detests the society of those whom the vulgar call 'ladies of position.' A woman—no matter how humble her birth—of genius; a clever woman; a woman who is well read without being a prig; a woman who is making a name for herself by her pen, her brush, her chisel, or by her musical attainments, is always sure of his homage and respectful admiration. In the society of such an one he thinks there is the best of all companionships, the companionship of thought; whilst on the other hand the society of ladies, of women who are simply the representatives of their order, and destitute of everything but modesty and good breeding, is in his opinion an unpleasant restraint. In the presence of the woman of Bohemia he can talk without reserve, he can consult his own comfort as to the posture he adopts, he can drink and smoke in her society without wounding her self-respect, and his brain becomes quick and teeming from the rapid interchange of ideas and the play of wit and humour. The propriety and inanities of a lady, however, freeze him up and render him dull and sulky. The Bohemian is, as a rule, singularly free from the scruples of the moralist and the antipathies of the bigot; he will make love to all who let him, and when he has money he intends to pay his debts. He is kind and generous—if it be in his power—to those who are not likely to develop into rivals; but where he fears competition he is more jealous and spiteful than would be expected from his jovial presence and careless indifference. He frequents those haunts in the town where he is sure to meet men of his own calling and addicted to his own tastes; and, except under certain special circumstances, he resents the intrusion of the followers of 'society' within his midst. In all things he consults his own ease, and refuses to hamper his pleasures by any restrictions which Mrs. Grundy may think it prudent to suggest.

He has little sympathy with certain of his brother

Bohemians, who are using the reputation which their productions have gained to become acquainted with the great and to hang on to the skirts of fashion. He ridicules their pretensions and despises their ambition. To him the conviviality of his own set, the freedom which permits each one to do as he pleases, the stories that are told, the liquor that is drunk, the fun and devilry which are interwoven with the texture of their lives, surpass all that the most servile toadyism can ever expect to obtain. Your true Bohemian is never more intolerant than when attacking those who are in a superior position to his own, and running amuck at all the proprieties. When by chance he meets a great man he will refute his arguments and disparage the profession to which he belongs. On the occasions when he treads upon that common ground where all worlds assemble—at flower-shows, exhibitions, musical and dramatic entertainments, and the rest—he is easily to be recognised by his garb and his studied contempt of all the *convenances* of life. Good-humoured enough in his own circle, a spirit of the most truculent antagonism pervades all his movements and conversation when he issues into a higher grade of life than his own. He thinks his own views upon all subjects to be correct, and is apt to become warm when contradicted. It is impossible to mistake him for aught than he is, or to identify him with the class to which he does not belong. In his dress and bearing we as plainly recognise him to be a citizen of the realm of Bohemia as we can tell the Frenchman who hails from Paris or the German whose home is in Berlin.

One such Bohemian is a member of the Caravanserai. Converts are always the most fervent in the support of their new creed, and no subjects are more patriotic than those who have been naturalised. Roy Somerset Fitzgerald Capel de Beaufoy (commonly called Alphabet de Beaufoy from his ample supply of Christian names) belongs to the Bohemian world, not by birth or profession, but by inclination and preference. The son of a distinguished Irish peer, who at one time gracefully filled the office of Viceroy of his native land, Alphabet de Beaufoy has little in common with the stock from which he has sprung. He is deficient in all the characteristics of the typical aristocrat. Little Farningham-West, with his blonde locks, his large blue eyes, his aquiline nose, his short upper-lip, and the smallness of his ears, hands, and feet, possesses in an eminent degree all those 'points' which race alone, it is said, can confer. Yet we know that he is but humbly born, and for the sake of Mrs. West, who is the severest of Sabbatarians, let us hope that the principles of ethnology occasionally vary in their course of development.

No one looking at Alphabet would imagine him to

belong to an exclusive order, and to be allied directly or indirectly to some of the proudest houses in the country. He is untidy in his dress, and careless as to the make and shape of his garments; as long as they

keep him warm in winter and cool in summer he is utterly indifferent as to their cut or texture. He has been reproved more than once by his sisters for putting in an attendance at a fashionable marriage with an alpaca coat on his back and a straw hat on his head, simply because the event happened to take place on a warm day in June. He abominates evening attire most heartily, and considers that as long as a man's linen is clean he is in proper costume to go anywhere. On the few occasions when he drives his stanhope in the Park, or rides his mare in the Row—for he prefers, not unwisely, the attractions of the suburbs—he dons a costume more suitable for the country than for London. Only once have I seen him in a tall hat, and then he told me he had been to church with his mother; but even this deference to the demands of civilisation was somewhat marred by the tweed suit he had thought it convenient to wear on the occasion.

There are some men who can dispense with all the advantages of art, but De Beaufoy is hardly to be included in the category. He is not ugly (no one with those honest brown eyes of his could be positively ill-looking, and some ladies have even been known to admit that he is 'almost handsome;' but then my friend has a very good fortune left him by his grandmother); but a man with a big nose, a large laughing mouth, a complexion very much freckled, hair thin and sandy, and a figure which good living and whisky-and-water have combined most effectually to destroy, should not be offended if his friends class him amongst the ill-favoured. Yet plain in appearance and disorderly in dress, it is impossible not to take the man for a gentleman after *speaking* to him. On certain occasions, when his self-respect has been wounded, his manner is very haughty and dignified; the great monarch himself could not be more crushing in his lofty disdain than De Beaufoy when he has to suppress a cad.

When Alphabet first joined the Caravanserai, it was considered 'shocking bad form' for him always to appear in the club in a wideawake, and to dine in a shooting-coat—it was treating the club like 'a pot-house,' some said; nor do I think such remarks were uncalled for by the supreme indifference of my friend to the conventionalities of life. Little West was one of the warmest of this band of critics; when, however, he discovered that the object of his severe strictures was the son of a mighty peer, he discontinued his observations, and did his best to become acquainted with the Bohemian. How elastic is human nature, and how much we forgive to our superiors! If Jones was to walk in the Park in a pot-hat, to enter the stalls of a theatre in a tweed suit, or to be seen outside an omnibus, he would lay himself open to being cut by his acquaintances. But if a noble Marquis dines at his club in thick boots and velveteens, or walks up St. James's-street eating walnuts, or is seen carrying home a large parcel from the Coöperative Stores, his conduct is not considered reprehensible. The one is 'a cad' for acting as he does; the other is praised for being above the 'timidity of the snob.' Who after this can say that there is not one law for the great and another for the humble?

Where civilisation has attained to its highest pitch of luxury and ostentation, as at the present day with us, there will always be men to whom its splendours and restraints will be distasteful. And as a rule those who can enjoy to the fullest extent all that a wealthy and refined civilisation has to offer will often be the very men to turn their backs upon its charms, and go elsewhere. These know what they are rejecting; they have entered the race, found the training irksome, and have seen that the prizes are not worth the winning. On the other hand, the men who have had little opportunity for the indulgence of social pleasures—either from the intensity of their industry or from obstacles that bar their progress in society—are always most keen in their pursuit of what wealth and rank can lay before them. The one have eaten the apple, and discovered that it is but Dead Sea fruit; the other see the pippin hanging on the tree —red, luscious, and tempting—and with outstretched hand and watering mouth long for the moment when they can grasp it and taste its imagined sweetness.

De Beaufoy has little to learn from the great world which he does not already know. Familiar from the days of his boyhood with all the seductions that society can offer, they cease now to have any attraction for him. It is with difficulty that he can ever be persuaded to be bored by going out to dance and dinner. His Bohemian tastes interfere sadly with his family ties, for it is only under the greatest pressure that he can be made to visit his relations, or to add himself to the number of the home circle. Yet if his mother and sisters only knew how easily he accepts an invitation from an actress to breakfast, or from an actor to supper, or from a detective to go the rounds of the cribs of London, they would scarcely feel flattered.

He is Bohemian to the backbone, and only cares for Bohemia. Every single haunt in the country of his adoption he is familiar with. When he is in society he is huffy, and stands on his dignity; outside its pale he will be on good terms with all the varied crew that cross his path. However strict may be the rules of a theatre, De Beaufoy has only to send his card round to the stage-door to be welcomed by the manager, to lounge about the greenroom, and to enter into little prandial arrangements with certain of the fair *artistes*. He belongs to a host of small clubs, which hold their meetings at a late hour of the night in cozy taverns, where the rooms are carpeted with sawdust; where the chairs are of the familiar Windsor pattern now relegated to kitchens;

where the tables are coverless, and of the darkest mahogany, and stained by the rings of pewter-pots and the blemishes caused by heated tumblers; where prints of famous trotters, of ex-champions of the belt and of the

river, of jockeys, statesmen, and deformities, hang against the walls; where the cuisine is strictly limited to kidneys, chops, and steaks, served with the whitest and most floury of potatoes; where the wines should be shunned, but where the beer and the spirits may be depended upon; and where the unfamed in letters and in art love to assemble. On the few occasions when it has been my good fortune to meet the magnates of authorship, I have invariably been disappointed with their powers of conversation. Their wit seems forced, their stories are old, and their talk is halting and hesitating, as if they knew that they were impostors, and on the point of being found out. In many an anteroom I have listened to far more wit and humour from men who could not write a page without committing themselves to errors in grammar and orthography.

Yet I must admit that when Alphabet has taken me into one of these obscure haunts as his guest, it has seldom been my lot to come away from the kindly dens disappointed. O those evenings, or rather nights, or rather mornings! How bright was the wit, how exquisitely droll, though somewhat naughty, the stories! how good were the songs! how jokes and (keen, but not malicious) chaff went the round! and how queer and uncouth were many of the members, and what a terrible dryness of throat seemed to afflict every one of the community! There they were—actors scarcely a remove from supers; journalists who were really little better than penny-a-liners; artists sketching for magazines, or painting for the dealers at famine prices; stage-managers of theatres one never heard of; authors who had to put their big thoughts away, and slave for the publishers as hacks; a few barristers who had never held a brief, but who, from their remarks, seemed worthy to occupy the seat on the bench vacated by an eminent Lord Chief Baron who at one time held his court in the Strand; one or two men whom drink had 'broke,' and who were picking up a livelihood as best they could; and a sprinkling of what some of the club called 'swells from the West-end.' What a motley lot! full of fun and devilry and brandy-and-water! They appeared to regard life as one gigantic joke, and to look upon him who was the funniest comedian as the best man amongst them. Never had I been made to laugh so much. The very appearance of some of the men, the expressions they used when discussing any question that came up, their wholesale irreverence for the leaders of their different professions, were all intensely amusing. Added to this, there was much real brilliancy in the conversation during the earlier part of the evening, till the talk unhappily became blended with spirits-and-water; whilst there were two men whose voices would have commanded high prices on the stage or in concert-rooms, could their sobriety only have been guaranteed. In such company even the great Dr. Johnson himself would have refrained from moralising. It is the next morning, when the tongue is parched and the brow is fevered, that we moralise. 'Those fellows *do* make me laugh,' said De Beaufoy, as we returned westwards; 'if we only had one or two of them at Pratt's!'

Reading a novel some nights ago, I was much

amused at certain ideas of the talented authoress touching Bohemia. The fair and gifted creature was evidently under the impression that there is a certain quarter in our capital which is as much the haunt of the Bohemian as Pall Mall is of the club-man. In this curious *faubourg*, we are told, the inhabitants consist entirely of artists, authors, journalists, actors, sculptors, and entertainers of the public. It has its own special clubs and taverns and places of amusement. None but the Bohemian is admitted within this privileged quarter; and it is subject to its own laws, which it has power to enforce by fine or punishment upon the refractory. I need hardly say that, except in the fertile imagination of the novelist, no such *imperium in imperio* exists.

As Satan in *Paradise Lost* is made to say that wherever he goes he makes a hell, so the Bohemian, wherever he pitches his tent, makes a Bohemia. Let De Beaufoy wander where he list, he is sure to surround himself with Bohemians. Though he flies the ensign of 'the Squadron,' he shuns all the fascinations of Cowes; but is generally to be found off the coast of Scotland or Ireland, where he is the patron of whalers, herring fishermen, coastguard-men, pilots, and the officials connected with the lighthouses and lifeboats. When becalmed or fond of a certain spot, he is a godsend to every one in the harbour, and to the seafaring community around. He gets up sailing-matches amongst the owners of the herring-smacks, rowing-matches and swimming-matches, and is most liberal in the distribution of prizes in the shape of tankards, kegs of whisky, ready money, and tablets of honeydew tobacco. Should a storm arise, and the lifeboat of the place distinguish itself, he invites the crew to a supper at a tavern, and shines as the most noisy and jovial of hosts. He avoids the country houses of the neighbourhood like the plague; but he can talk by the hour to an old salt, and is the best and thirstiest listener imaginable to a yarn. Alphabet is no fool or 'chalk yachtsman.' He has studied harder in Thames-street than most men do at the University, and has obtained his certificate from the Board of Trade. The sailors know that, though he is a 'swell,' he is as smart an amateur seaman as there is afloat; and captains of barques have more than once been indebted to him for downright professional assistance.

Like many men passionately fond of the sea, Alphabet is but a lukewarm lover of the pleasures of the chase. He has a little hunting-box about fifty miles from London; and if a bad rider to hounds, he is at least a bold one, for he cranes at nothing, though he has come terribly to grief on more than one occasion. When a frost sets in, I fancy he is not keenly disappointed; for at such times he drives over to the stables of a neighbouring trainer of great repute, and is far happier chatting with that gentleman over some old dry sherry, hearing anecdotes about the days of the turf past and present, inspecting the horses, and talking to the jockeys, than when pursuing the wily fox. He is a good shot, but in his eyes there is no sport more attractive than at the dead of night to join with the keepers in a free-fight with the poachers. Those guardians of the game for miles around always let 'the honourable' know when they expect battle, and seldom does he fail to put in an appearance. Some men have a weakness for driving locomotives, others for attending conflagrations and working the fire-engine, and others for slaving at a printing-press. The weakness of De Beaufoy is a moonlight night, the rides of a wood, and a hand-to-hand encounter between a dozen men and a dozen poachers. It is fortunate for the poachers that the law limits Alphabet's powers of punishment as a magistrate, else those sneaking purloiners would never receive a more lenient sentence than five years' penal servitude.

Whenever an opportunity presents itself De Beaufoy runs up to London. Like your true Bohemian, he is always happy in a crowd, with the bustle of life going on around him, the fun of the fair presenting itself at every step, agitation, noise, confusion, amusement at every turn. The theatre is his favourite pastime, and he must be on the high seas, or else there must be very good reason for his absence, when he fails to attend the performances of a first night. He is extremely fond of discovering obscure talent, and more than one young actor owes his elevation to the London boards to the interest and discrimination of my friend, who has been struck by his playing in the provinces. Sunday is the favourite day for De Beaufoy to give his dinners at the Caravanserai, because that day is generally the only one at the disposal of the actors, who are sure to be amongst his guests. There is scarcely a theatre in town where his presence is not welcome in the greenroom, and there is not a play brought out but that he forms part of the audience which listens to its first reading. Intimately acquainted with modern dramatic literature, De Beaufoy would make an excellent newspaper critic were he forced to write for his living. More than once, at some of his tavern haunts, have I heard him, after the first night of a new piece, correcting the surmises of dramatic critics as to the source of the new play, showing what was original in it and what was plagiarised, and giving chapter and verse for his authority. Actresses like him, not simply because he is very generous and peculiarly susceptible to the charms of a pretty face and of a well-moulded figure, but because, having travelled much, and having been acquainted with most of the leading actors in Europe, he has been really of service to them in the creation of their characters. I know one young actress who made a great hit in a part, and yet her idea of the character was due, not to the originality of her genius, but solely to the teaching of De Beaufoy, who had seen when at Dresden an obscure German actress in a *rôle* of a similar kind.

Anything new, or any one who is making a sensation,

is sure of finding in De Beaufoy a patron and friend. Is a comic singer the rage, is a gymnast particularly clever on the trapeze, has a pedestrian made himself famous by his walking powers, has a new comic author appeared, Alphabet will make his acquaintance, and if the man is presentable ask him to supper at a certain excellent hostel not a hundred miles from Covent Garden. Is there a man or woman noted for gigantic stature, enormous bulk, or some extraordinary malformation, De Beaufoy is sure to be among those present at the earliest medical investigation. His curiosity is boundless. He visits prisons, lunatic asylums, convict establishments, and, thanks to the protection of friendly detectives, he knows every thieves' kitchen in London as well as if he had lived all his years in the atmosphere of Scotland Yard. The low life of the town, the society of those in an inferior grade to his own, intercourse with that great body of the community whose object it is to amuse the public by their peculiar gifts, have attractions for him which are irresistible. His fortune, his name, his social surroundings, have placed him in the order of the patricians; but in tastes, habits, and sympathies nature has marked him out as a proletarian. As the age of miracles is past it cannot be expected that he will ever be transformed into other than he is. He will live and die a Bohemian.

A PARASITE.

A PARASITE.

In the animal world there are certain insects, apparently of little use in the scheme of creation except to themselves, which derive their sustenance entirely from the objects, whether animate or inanimate, to which they cling. Refusing to be shaken off, they only take their departure when the victim of their close embraces has yielded up all that he, she, or it once possessed. Their appearance upon the scene is generally indicative of two things: the first, that the creature upon which they settle is a prey worth the sucking; and the second, that their attentions generally end in the ruin of their subject. We know the plant that stealthily creeps up the stalwart trunk of the vigorous tree twines its deadly foliage around the bark, and soon causes what was once blossom and vitality to be transformed into tinder and decay. We know the insidious reptile which so tenaciously adheres to its quarry, that, whilst it swells and battens upon the blood, every prick of its sucker inflicts a mortal wound. We know that terrible excrescence, half animal, half vegetable, which, wherever it deposits itself, becomes so identified with the object of its selection as to be an actual necessity to the existence of the victim: remove it, and he dies; starve it, and he perishes; the two—the victimiser and the victimised—are inseparable until the hateful union is dissolved by the triumph of the parasite.

Nor is the species unknown to the social world. Varied in its operations, of different tastes, habits, and capacity, the manœuvres of the class are always the same in the end—profit to themselves and destruction to the creature fixed upon for suction. As in animal life, so in social life, the parasite never attaches itself to a vigorous and healthy subject. It knows that where there is sound and genuine vitality it has no place, and would be instantly expelled did it attempt to take up its abode. Its scent is keen after physical or moral decay, and where that is found it is sure of a home. The oak may appear to the uninitiated healthy and flourishing; but the parasite knows what poison is instilled in the juice of the sap, and how long it will be before the branches wither, and the trunk be the haunt of corruption. The man may seem, to most of his acquaintance, more than ordinarily free from the faults of human nature; yet the parasite knows what are his infirmities, and settles upon the weak points, provided something worth the effort may be extracted from them.

The social parasite is of all descriptions; the genus is as extensive as ubiquitous; still its characteristics are invariably the same—to maintain its existence at the expense of another.

There is the literary parasite. He may be of a keenly acquisitive turn of mind, and obtain his reputation by sucking the brains of deceased authors, of obsolete authors, of unknown foreign authors, or of authors who have innocently confided their manuscripts to his hands, and, by manipulating their thoughts and dressing their ideas in a different costume, pose before the public as a new and original writer. A great work of science appears; it is the result of the labour of half a lifetime; it is heavy, crude, and undigested, and appeals to the few. The literary parasite takes it up, cleverly evades infringing upon its copyright, and popularises it; it has a large sale, and the parasite profits at the expense of the discoverer. A valuable history is published; he epitomises it. A writer hits the public taste by ingenuity of plot or charm of style; he copies it. It may be that the parasite has been unfortunate in his productions; they have no market; they are unread at the libraries; they have been bought by weight by the butterman and the trunkmaker. The instincts of his species prompt him how to act. He fastens himself upon some writer who has gained for himself a great name. He criticises with spiteful malevolence every work such an author produces. He discovers errors in his dates, in his grammar, in his transcripts, in all that he says and thinks. When the great author issues his volumes, the cynical and malicious rush to the reviews and the magazines to hear what the parasite has to say. Abuse, so long as it be bitter and personal, never lacks readers. As the moon receives all her light from the sun, so the literary parasite borrows all his lustre from the great intellectual orbs he copies or traduces.

There is the commercial parasite. He attaches himself to some great capitalist, sings the praises of his wealth, vaunts the undertakings he has set afloat, and receives his reward by sneaking into the board-room as a director. He makes it his business to know when a bank is shaky in its credit, or a stock-jobber has sold shares which he cannot deliver, and forthwith it is through him and his tribe that the stock of the one falls to the ground, and the stock of the other rises to a heavy premium. He twines himself round the great pillars of the City, and is always petitioning for 'tips,' and for allotments in new Companies which are sure on their day of issue to be quoted at a profit. When one of his patrons fails, or is committed for fraudulent proceedings, the parasite is always among the first to say that 'he knew all along that the firm was rotten,' or that 'the fellow was the greatest scoundrel unhung.' He worships chairmen of committees, for he is a great respecter of the powers that be. He is the toady of the wealthy merchant, but the systematic libeller of all the smaller fry. He is the Ananias of panics, and would lie till his tongue cleaved to his mouth, provided he could rig the market so as to serve his ends. He is the first to crave for time when unable to meet his own bills, and the last to extend such mercy to another.

There is the political parasite. He clings to the leaders of the party, writes them up in newspapers, and flatters them at the meetings of their associations. He gets up testimonials; he is honorary secretary to half a dozen political institutions, but leaves the work to a clerk; he is the terror of private secretaries, upon whom he is always calling; he is the author of pamphlets, which he sends to every member of the Cabinet, on all the great public questions; and he passes his fussy days in the hope that he will eventually creep into office and fifteen hundred a year. If he is appointed, the country is saved. If the Government refuse to recognise his claims, the country is going to the mischief, and he offers his services to the other side.

There is the military parasite, haunting the Horse Guards, and cringing after good civil or military posts, to the exclusion of men who have served their country in all parts of the globe, whilst he himself has never been out of England. There is the clerical parasite, hanging on to the dignitaries of the Church; toadying private patrons, pretending to interest himself in the

labours of the great religious societies, fawning, scheming, eating dirt, and crawling in the dust, provided he only succeeds in obtaining the prize he has set before him—a good fat living. There is the scientific parasite, turning the inventions of other men to his own account, and stealing the principle of their ideas, whilst keeping himself clear of the Patent Laws. And there is the commonest and most prosperous of the order—the parasite who makes society his victim.

Scrope Hillingdon is a prominent member of this class of creature. A younger son, he testifies by his life and career to the partialities of the law of primogeniture. Whilst his brother, Sir Alured, is a great landowner and a county magnate of the wealthiest and most powerful description, Scrope is a nobody, and lord of some six thousand pounds, strictly tied up, which yield him four and a half per cent per annum. During his father's lifetime no distinction was made between himself and the heir. Both went to the same school; both went to the same tutor on the Continent; both spent the same pocket-money; and both, on their return to the parental roof, led the same kind of lives. Scrope thought of entering a profession; but pleasant years passed by, and he forgot all about his intention. He lived in the same set as his elder brother; went into the same society; belonged to the same clubs; had the same tastes, and indulged in the same expenditure; when he wanted horses he drew upon the paternal stables, and when he wanted funds he was permitted to draw upon the paternal banker. One chill October morning his father dies; the elder son succeeds to the family honours; and the younger son finds himself with a pittance, on which he is to live for the rest of his days.

What course is open to him? His past habits and tastes have unfitted him for the slow laborious business of following a profession and making it pay. He has lived in society, he has been accustomed to luxuries of a certain kind which have developed into necessities, and whenever he wanted the sinews of war 'the old dad parted like a trump.' Therefore, without any previous training in self-denial or economy, he suddenly finds himself thrown upon the world a beggar. All the accomplishments he possesses are useless for the serious purposes of life; it is hard work tilling land with a silver trowel. He can ride; he can dance; he is a fair shot; he can read French; he is a very good amateur vet.; and his knowledge of navigation, for a yachtsman, is more than respectable. Yet, desirable as these accomplishments are for the idle man, they have no market value. To fight the battle of life a man wants something more than a becoming uniform.

Scrope soon realised his position. His brother was very kind to him, was hospitality itself in the way of putting him up in the country for any length of period, allowed him to ride his horses, lent him his yacht and paid all the expenses; but he drew the line at ready money. When Scrope hinted at his wretched allowance, and how acceptable a further provision would be to him, Sir Alured never rose to the bait. On the contrary, it was the baronet who made out that his own resources were crippled—he had to pay off certain heavy mortgages; the portions of his sisters were a terrible charge upon the estate; the expenses that he had incurred for drainage and building improvements were simply enormous; the demands of his tenants were as incessant as they were exorbitant; and the rest of the usual excuses which country gentlemen make when directly applied to by any branch of their family for money. Sir Alured would do all in his power to help his brother; he would willingly use what interest he possessed with the Government to get him an appointment. How would he like an inspectorship of factories, or the governorship of a prison, or a post in the Consular service? But he clearly made him to understand that the property would not bear the grant of any addition to the six thousand pounds, and that he would not consider himself liable for any debts that the younger brother might in the future incur.

For a man of Scrope's tastes to live on an income of something less than three hundred a year was practically impossible. With economy it might keep him in clothes and dinners, and suffice for his travelling expenses, but it was incapable of further extension. He thought of the matrimonial market: but heiresses, numerous and amiable enough in novels, are not so easily found in real life to bestow their wealth upon penniless younger sons.

Gradually, and almost unconsciously, Scrope sank to the vocation of a parasite. He had birth, he had good looks, and, above all, thanks to his name and his sisters' marriages, he was in society. Around him he saw many men who had what he had not, and who coveted to possess what he, until he was made to learn its value, held somewhat cheap. With these people he entered into a treaty of reciprocity; he gave what they desired, he received what he was in need of.

The acquaintance of Scrope is strictly limited to those who are calculated to be of service to him. As sure as he attaches himself to any man or family, so sure is it that the victim is worth the bleeding. A young peer has just succeeded to his property; Scrope makes his acquaintance, takes stock of his intellectual attainments, and if he finds him a likely subject to be operated upon, proceeds at once to leech him. Endowed with most of those agreeable qualities which captivate the young, Scrope soon weaves his cobwebs to catch his fly. He flatters the lad about the two points that youth is the most easily gulled—the fair sex and horse-flesh. My lord soon fancies himself a perfect lady-killer, and is introduced by Scrope into doubtful society; and, as a consummate judge of that noble animal the horse, buys from his friend at high prices the refuse of the market. The parasite is generally a good card-player, and Scrope is no exception to the rule. He teaches the young aristocrat how to play whist and *écarté*, and the subtle beauties that are to be found in baccarat, napoleon, and poker. Such lessons are not given, as we are aware, for nothing; and perhaps most of us have had to pay pretty heavily for our knowledge in these matters. I should like to know the extent of the cheques to which many a young peer has scrawled his name and handed over to Scrope as fees for tuition.

The next move of the parasite is to look after the estates of his victim; and, if he finds the steward is capable of being corrupted, the two stand in together, and derive no inconsiderable profit from what they are pleased to term the management of the property. During this happy period of suction Scrope has seldom occasion to touch the interest upon his six thousand pounds. His lordship provides him with all that ministers to the wants of man, and as long as such a state of things continues Scrope is perfectly content and supremely loyal. The intimacy, however, seldom lasts for any great length of time. Many causes operate against its duration. The victim gradually finds out, perhaps, that he is being pigeoned, and a rupture takes place; or he marries, and his wife disapproves of the acquaintance of Mr. Hillingdon; or his friends interfere; or he ends by being ruined, when it is the parasite and not the peer who brusquely dissolves partnership.

Scrope, however, has many irons in the fire, and if one falls out it is soon replaced. To the man of trade whose wife is ambitious of social honours the parasite is a most invaluable friend. He tones down the gaudiness of the furniture, and alters the suburban look of the appointments of the establishment. He gives little hints as to behaviour and deportment, which are gratefully received. He examines the lady's visiting-list, and freely erases from it. When his lessons have been mastered sufficiently, so that the woman can dress herself without courting ridicule, and the man can behave at dinner without attracting attention, Scrope calls upon his sisters and desires them 'to be civil to these people.' And those fair dames, knowing that it is to their brother's interest to comply with his request, carry out his instructions to the letter. More than one eminent City lady has entered society through the interest of the female branches of the Hillingdon family in her behalf, and more than one eminent City man has had to pay substantial footing-money to Scrope for the favours thus accorded.

Scrope is the middle-man between the outside world and the inside world, and, provided you pay his fees, he will do the best he can for you. As there are men in London who will furnish you with cooked dinners, with active waiters, with bands (brass or string), with plate and china, and temporary decorations of all kinds, so Scrope will supply you with guests for your garden-parties, celebrities for your dinners, and saltatory youth for your dances. It is like everything else nowadays, only a question of arrangement—and ready money. If it may be said without offence, I should certainly decline to appoint Scrope Hillingdon as one of my executors; I should not recommend him as a trustee; there are times when his word might be open to suspicion; it might be perhaps carrying confidence too far to lend him money; but if I wanted a garden-party to be a success, or the dresses at a fancy-ball to be noted for their artistic or picturesque character, or a complicated cotillon to be got up, or pleasant people to be collected together and to be amused, or anything of a similar nature, I should without hesitation be only too glad to employ the services of Scrope. He is a kind of master of the ceremonies let out for hire.

Nor is he in this matter different from the rest of the class. One of the oddest features which society nowadays presents is the calm business-like manner in which certain of its members, without apparent loss of caste, receive money for the display of any accomplishments they may possess. You go to one house, and listen to a young man pleasantly warbling at the piano to a hushed crowd, and your hostess tells you in a whisper that he is very much in request, and that she pays him ten guineas for his three songs. The next evening you are at dinner, and there opposite you is the young man, whom in the simplicity of your heart you regarded as an ordinary professional vocalist, and you find that he is an officer retired from the service, and the nephew of a bishop. At a third house you meet a mediæval designer; at a fourth, a comic entertainer; at a fifth, a reader; at a sixth, an amateur actor, and so on,—all young men of the most irreproachable connections, all 'in society,' and all who receive payment in solid cash for their services. It is difficult in these days to know where the amateur ends and the professional begins. In former times the line of demarcation was very fairly drawn; he who received payment for his work could no longer dub himself amateur. But now it is notorious that men, who would be much angered if they were considered as professionals, sing at drawing-rooms for money, act at private theatricals for money, give comic or dramatic readings for money, ride indirectly for money, play cricket-matches for money, superintend the decoration of your houses in the most approved style of Gothic art for money; and soon, I suppose, country gentlemen, who wish to outrival each other in the slaughter they can effect, will have to pay crack shots to walk their moors and enter their preserves; or hostesses, in despair at the absence of good dancers, will have to pay young men to waltz. Fifty years ago such a nondescript state of things would not have been permitted to exist. If a man chose to be a 'professional,' he had to work at his career as a professional; if he became celebrated, society was glad to know him; if he failed to attain distinction, he was lost to his former set. But it would never have been allowed for a man to expect the social advantages of an amateur whilst in the enjoyment of the pecuniary rewards of the professional. We in this generation are more liberal; we permit our young men to serve society and worship Mammon.

Such being the case, Scrope Hillingdon has carved out for himself a very lucrative career as an amateur master of the ceremonies. To the great and the wealthy, whom he knows, he takes an amazing amount of trouble off their hands. He organises their picnics, superintends all the arrangements at their garden-parties, prompts the nervous and the hesitating at private theatricals, gives instructions as to the dresses to be worn at fancy-balls, makes neat little speeches when circumstances require them; and, in short, is a kind of general-utility man on the stage of society. Of course he is paid. If the truth were known, that paternal legacy of six thousand pounds must have swelled itself into quite a splendid array of figures by this time. I cannot say that the course he pursues is either pleasant or highly honourable, but it is eminently prosperous. Young men have entered life under his auspices: some have shunned the rocks ahead, and got safe into port; others have struck and have foundered: but Scrope Hillingdon, the wrecker, has managed, ere the bark went down, to secure for himself a goodly portion of the cargo. Wealthy men have been ushered into society through the *portières* of his sisters' drawing-rooms; their ambitious wives have entered upon a reckless career of luxury and display; ruin has overtaken them; yet Scrope Hillingdon has made full profit out of the transaction before the servants were dismissed, and the petition in bankruptcy filed.

As in the days of fable story there were few who crossed the path of the ogre but had to pay for their temerity, so there are few who have fallen in the way of Scrope and have escaped unhurt. He may not have taken their lives, but at least his victims issue from his den torn and maimed. Why was poor young Fluffe, Lord Downy's eldest son, the gayest Lancer that ever fluttered pennon, hurriedly obliged to send in his papers? Had Scrope nothing to do with introducing the lad to the money-lenders, and with the history of that card scandal which was the talk of every ante-room in the kingdom? What made poor old Molasses, that eminent sugar-baker, suspend payment and appear in the *Gazette*? Was it not the extravagance of his wife, prompted and encouraged by Scrope? and pray how much of that misspent wealth found its way into Scrope's pocket? Why did young Fitz-Storke have to mortgage the Heron property to the hilt? Who was the cause of Monty Lascelles having to resign his excellent appointment, and betake himself to cattle-farming at Monte Video? Who created

the difference between young Palmer and his father, and who was the real cause why that ill-balanced youth imitated the signature of his parent? Where are Arthur Domville, Reggie Turner, the 'General,' Jumping Hinton, and the rest of that gay crew? Broke, helplessly broke! And their ruin, either directly or indirectly, lies at the door of Scrope Hillingdon.

Naturally there are numerous stories against this plausible gentleman, yet none have been proved in such a satisfactory manner as to justify either society or the committee of his clubs to take cognisance of his proceedings. On the contrary, on the few occasions when it has been necessary to make some quiet and unofficial inquiry into certain matters with which Scrope was connected, he has come triumphantly out of the investigation, and those who have set it on foot have been made to smart for their suspicions. Still most of us know it bodes little good to the aristocrat or plutocrat who is seen much in his society. How we pity the young men he collects around his luxurious dining-table at the club, who laugh at his stories in the smoking-room, who sit in his box at the theatre, and who are so proud to be seen with a man who knows everybody, and one of whose sisters is a countess of the highest fashion! Rest assured that a time will come when his victims will find neither his dinners appetising nor his stories amusing, but, when that grave parliament with the family lawyer is held, will curse the day they ever allowed themselves to be dazzled by the brilliancy of the gifts of Scrope Hillingdon.

Of late years this skilful spider has chiefly been content with spinning his web in commercial circles. He is just the man the wealthy trader admires. He is a gentleman by birth, and looks the character; his manners are perfect, he knows everybody who is worth knowing,

and he is entirely free from pride. Given a man of undoubted wealth, and there are few who can surpass Scrope in all the arts of fascination; to the ordinary mortal he is, however, as a rule, cold and repellent. The plutocrat likes to have Scrope at his house, and to trot him out to the different guests. 'Know that fellow? O, he's a capital chap! He is a brother of Sir Alured Hillingdon' (occasionally Sir Halured Illingdon), 'and his sister, don't you know, is the wife of that old swell, the Earl of Mountsorrel. O, he's a great friend of mine; always here.' And as long as the plutocrat has a large balance at his banker's, a good house over his head, a good cook in his kitchen, curious vintages in his cellar, a well-kept country house, a moor to shoot over, a deer-forest, and perhaps a steam-yacht, Scrope has not the slightest objection to be his 'great friend.' Indeed, he prefers the plutocracy to the aristocracy. 'They think more of one, and they give better dinners,' he says. After a few weeks' acquaintance with Mr. Bullion, the old game begins. 'I suppose you know that Lady Mountsorrel is my sister?' asks Scrope of his host, as they sit together after dinner. 'O, of course; who does not?' is the reply. 'Why, she is one of the most fashionable women in London.' 'I was thinking,' says Scrope carelessly, 'of asking her to call upon Mrs. Bullion. Your wife would have no objection, I suppose?' 'Objection, my dear feller! Why, it's what Mrs. Bullion has been badgering me about for the last—I mean my wife would take it as a great honour, Mr. Hillingdon, and I should be very much obliged to you. You know Mrs. Bullion is a bit '*igh* in her notions.' Then the conversation takes the form of business. At the end of a few days the barouche of Lady Mountsorrel appears at the door of Mr. Bullion's mansion; cards are handed out; Mrs. Bullion, seated in the gaudiest of chariots drawn by the showiest of horses in the brassiest of harness, returns the visit; and a fortnight afterwards the couple are asked to dinner. Scrope is invited to meet them; he takes down Mrs. Bullion, and freely introduces her at the reception which his sister afterwards holds. He *borrows* (that is the polite way of putting it) a loan from Mr. Bullion shortly after this arrangement has been entered into.

The system of 'promotion by purchase' has been transferred from the ranks of the army to the ranks of society.

AGITATION.

AGITATION.

The professional fanner of discontent has at the present day a wide and active career before him. Scarcely a question arises which is not capable of bringing grist to his mill. No matter what be the course proposed by the calm and temperate mind for the solution of surrounding difficulties, the agitator is equal to the occasion, and can discover flaws in every scheme. In a country like England, where there is great wealth on the one side, and great poverty on the other,—where labour and capital, production and want, free-trade and restrictions are ever coming into collision,—it is not difficult for the man whose interest it is to sow the seeds of dissension to scatter them broadcast, and to watch the upgrowth of a goodly crop.

The agitator declines to be satisfied, and can turn the softest answer into bitterness. If we extend the suffrage, we are permitting an ignorant majority to overawe an educated minority. If we refuse to extend the suffrage, we are allowing a coterie to legislate for the nation, and ignoring the opinions of the masses. If we reduce the naval and military estimates, we are enfeebling our position as a great power. If we increase the estimates, we are wantonly adding to the taxation of the country. If we take part in the affairs of foreign nations, we are guilty of officious interference. If we hold ourselves aloof, we are conscious of our insignificance. If we consent to arbitration, we are afraid to fight. If we are prepared to maintain our demands by force, we are a blustering bully. If we add new laws to the statute-book, we are harassing the country by over-legislation. If we cease to legislate, we are indifferent to the existence of the grossest abuses. If we advise capital to modify its gains, we are being intimidated by the working classes. If we recommend labour to succumb, we are pandering to the extortions of a grinding plutocracy. Nothing that we do or suggest satisfies the agitator, whose object it is to fan the flames to heat himself.

Outside the realm of agitation the professional agitator has nothing, and has attained to no distinction. Discontent is the atmosphere he breathes, and he lives only by encouraging the passions and prejudices of his followers. He is indifferent to what cause he supports, provided he sees his way to bringing his name before the public, to becoming the agent of the special societies that have been created, and to being handsomely paid for his services. He may pose as the uncompromising defender of Protestant principles, flood the land with offensive literature, and incite mob-riots by the stimulating invective of his lectures. He may appear in the garb of a Ritualist, and derive a handsome annuity, thanks to the subscriptions of sympathisers, out of the prosecutions that have been instituted against him. He may stand forth as the fierce denunciator of the wrongs of the working man, and draw a comfortable salary out of the penny contributions of the masses. If there is an explosion underground, he depicts the sufferings of the poor miner, and exposes the indifference of the Government to the welfare of the mining population. If a ship is lost at sea, he dilates upon the scoundrelism of ship-owners, who, provided they obtain their insurance, are careless as to the soundness of the craft they overload with cargo, or the safety of the crew they collect together. If there is a strike, he sides with the foes of the manufacturer, coal-owner, or agricultural employer. If men, notorious for their political offences, or for their fraudulent practices, are confined in gaol, he takes their part, speaks at indignation meetings, drives in a fly at Sunday processions, and is incessant in petitioning the Home Secretary. The aim of his mischievous existence is to be always talked about, to have his name always cropping up in newspapers, and to create, if not an anxiety, at least a curiosity, in the mind of the public as to his movements during seasons of crisis and excitement.

The goal that the professional agitator sets before him varies according to his talents, his position in life, and the notoriety he succeeds in obtaining. At the end of a few years, what with contributions, peculations, fees for lecturing, and the sale of pamphlets, he may be able to retire on his ill-gotten gains and quit the trade of agitation for ever. Or he may receive an income from his followers, have his political expenses paid, and enter Parliament. Or it may be the policy of Government to throw him a sop in the shape of petty office, and silence his barking. But whatever be the prizes of the seditious career that the professional agitator has chosen, of one thing we may be assured, that no sooner has he received the reward that contents him, than he will utterly ignore in the future the advocacy of the cause that has borne him on its tide to success. Of what use is the orange when its contents have been well sucked? Job knew human nature well when he wrote, 'Doth the wild-ass bray when it hath grass?'

There is one man of my acquaintance who, when he finds his way into the Caravanserai, is generally to be seen in the library poring over the pages of Hansard or the file of old newspapers, who on the whole has not found the profession of agitation either dull or unprosperous. There is no mistaking Bob Royston for other than he is. Who but a demagogue and the favourite tribune of the people would dare be seen, west of Charing Cross, wearing that low, broad-brimmed, conspirator's-looking hat, and with that huge, ill-folded, faded, green umbrella as a staff for his footsteps? Who but an agitator—one so absorbed in the miseries of the people as to be heedless of the *petits soins* of civilisation —would wear so rusty and shapeless a coat, so unbuttoned a waistcoat, such terribly curtailed inexpressibles, and such ragged and discoloured linen? Who but a democrat could knit his features into so severe a frown, and pass his hand through his long untidy locks with such an air of thought, menace, contempt, and ferocity? Who but the poor man's advocate could enter the club, and so savagely glare at the luxurious surroundings of the Caravanserai; at the newspapers stitched and carefully folded for perusal; at the oil-lamps giving a soft subdued light; at the sofas and easy-chairs, so suggestive of conversation, repose, or slumber; at the attentive gentle-footed waiters, wearing the plush and stockings of servitude; at the hush and quiet of well-disciplined arrangements? He says, as plainly as face can speak without words, 'Ye Sybarites, ye pampered scions of a one-sided state of creation, why are ye revelling in luxury and in all the refinements of the most selfish civilisation, whilst yonder, outside these walls, are the bitterest misery, the most grinding poverty, the basest crime? Arouse ye out of your sloth, and come out and

help us!' And who but the agitator, born to be obeyed by his followers, to be listened to with deference, and to be enveloped in the incense of homage and flattery, could so bully the waiters who have to attend upon his orders—could so rudely crush conversation by the introduction of argument—could be so arrogant, offensive, and generally disagreeable?

There is in all that Royston does that charming suavity of the Republican who considers rudeness a proof of independence, and that good manners and servility necessarily go hand in hand together. He talks in a loud voice, as if he were addressing a meeting; he snatches a newspaper from your knee without apology; he jostles you on one side as he enters the room; he breathes hard as he writes his letters; he opens the window when the wind is in the east; he disturbs the silence of the library by his snores, and the waiters dare not awake him; he eats like a German, and drinks spirits-and-water like an exciseman. He is one of the most objectionable men in the club, yet neither the club nor the committee can turn him out. Ah, if clubs could only treat offensive persons as they do bankrupts, how much more pleasant those institutions would become! But, then, who are to decide as to the offensive people? We might have a club which would winnow its members till none were left.

Yet there was a time when Royston was deemed a good fellow, and no one who knew him in the days of his youth would have imagined that he would have developed into the turbulent truculent man he now is. At Winchester he was a popular captain of the school, and when he went up to New, his rooms, owing to his musical talents and the liberality of his festivities, were among the most frequented in the University. It was only when he quitted Oxford, and after several years passed in obscurity at the Bar, that he began to pose as the people's friend and the enemy of his own class. As so often happens to men who have attained to distinction or to notoriety, a purely accidental circumstance made him create the character he now plays with such success upon life's stage. How chance fashions the careers of men! Had Smeaton been articled to an attorney, would the world ever have heard of him? Had Rousseau taken his seat at the paternal cobbler's stall, should we have had the *Confessions* and *Emile?* Had Hume gone into trade, would our literature have been enriched with his History? Had Turner remained a barber, would he have been handed down to posterity as the Shakespeare of English landscape-painters? Had Lord Eldon betaken himself to coals instead of to Coke upon Littleton, would he ever have raised himself above the ruck of mankind? Had the great Thesiger remained in the navy, should we ever have heard of his name? And if Royston had not been engaged as counsel in a leading case, would he ever have achieved notoriety and developed into a mob-hero? Fortune in one of her freaks made him what he is, and transformed him from what he was.

There is no necessity to enter into the details of the famous trial which a few years ago was the talk of the country, and still occupies a prominent place among our *causes célèbres*. A Roman Catholic peer had succeeded in forcing his orphan niece, to whom he was guardian, to be converted from Protestantism, to place her fortune in his hands, and to enter a convent. The friends of the lady interfered, and, on discovering that the young woman had acted under severe pressure in alienating her property and in changing her religion, demanded her release, and the restoration of her estates. His lordship, however, denied the facts brought against him, and declined to return a single acre of what he was pleased to term 'the free and spontaneous gift of his niece.' The case came into court, and Royston held a brief as counsel for the young lady. As luck would have it, his leader became so gravely indisposed during the proceedings that almost the whole onus of the trial devolved upon the junior. Royston saw his opportunity, embraced it, and became famous. The case had all those elements which appeal to the passions and prejudices of the multitude. The oppressor was a peer, a man of wealth, and a Papist; the victim was a young and pretty woman, compelled to abjure her religion, and to be immured against her will in that ecclesiastical prison, a convent. Fierce were the denunciations of

Royston against the avarice and inutility of an aristocracy, against the inhumanity of the defendant, and the diabolical nature of the machinery of the Romish Church when it was once set in motion to crush a helpless victim! With what keenness he cross-examined the Roman Catholic bishops and monsignors and lady-superiors and nuns that appeared in the witness-box, and how terrible was his invective when he commented upon their proceedings! How eloquently he discoursed upon the virtues of the plaintiff, her miseries, her sufferings, and the tyranny of her protector, who had robbed her of her property, and alienated her from those of her religion!

The trial was eagerly watched by the public. All classes of society were interested in it, and the court was densely crowded throughout the proceedings. The newspapers took the matter up, and their columns were filled with verbatim reports of each day's doings. Seldom had a barrister such an opportunity, and Royston made the most of it. He was the idol of the hour, and both when he entered and took his departure from Westminster Hall he was vociferously cheered by an admiring crowd. When the verdict of the jury was given in favour of his fair client the enthusiasm of the mob knew no bounds; they applauded in open court, they surrounded Royston as he entered his brougham, and if the police had not interfered they would have taken the job-horses out and drawn the carriage themselves.

Before that memorable trial Royston was unknown; after it not a hamlet in the country but was familiar with his name. Suddenly, without preparation, and almost in spite of himself, the barrister had created a *rôle* which he felt henceforth he must always act. Before the trial he had been welcome in society; he had, as a gentleman, lived amongst gentlemen, and he had entertained the views and sentiments of the class to which he, by birth, belonged. All was now changed. Carried away by the homage of the mob, he had, during the trial, identified himself with the people; he had uttered sentiments which he knew would be popular with the crowd; he had inveighed against the governing classes, against the inequality in the distribution of wealth, against the absorption of the land by a pleasure-seeking aristocracy, against the Romish Church, and much that he had said against the Church of Rome was applicable to the Church of England. Yet whilst indulging in these diatribes against the upper classes he had pandered to the vanity and the discontent of the mob, by applauding all their actions and sympathising with all their grievances.

There was now no alternative but for him to continue as he had begun. He had insulted society, and the polite world looked askant at him; his former friends shunned him as a political mischief-maker; save one or two very advanced Radicals, he was cut by all who had once known him. Indifferent to all slights, Royston

threw in his lot with the most mischievous of the lower orders—with the men who will agitate, but who will not work. By these he was most cordially welcomed. He was on the committees of all their societies for the equalisation of mankind and the destruction of capital.

In all their differences he was appointed their arbitrator. He was the favourite speaker at all their meetings. A newspaper called the *Red Banner* was especially started to report his speeches, and to convey his opinions to the multitude. Whenever an agitation deputation — no matter what was the cause of the agitation — waited upon the Home Secretary or other Minister, Royston was the spokesman. The mob, whatever be its faults, is seldom fickle in its loyalty to its own favourites; come weal or woe, through pleasure or persecution, in storm or sunshine, the fervent ignorant crowd declines to be laughed out of its sympathies, or to depose the idols it has once set up. Politicians, newspapers, reviews, priests, dandies, might sneer at Royston, but his unwashed adherents never doubted his judgment or deserted his standard. In all strikes, lock-outs, and agricultural differences, his opinion was the first asked and the first followed.

The forensic career presents numerous phases of existence. There is the barrister who wins a name as a brilliant lawyer, who enters Parliament, who becomes one of the law-advisers of the Crown, and who ends by gaining the great prizes of his profession. There is the barrister who, as the son of a solicitor or as the husband of the daughter of a solicitor, finds himself at once the master of a lucrative practice, and though he may never have been heard of by the public outside, yet he is not the least amongst the luminaries of his calling. There is the barrister who, despairing of solicitors' visits, betakes himself to the cheaper but readier rewards of journalism. There is the barrister, generally the son of a retired tradesman, who is called to the Bar because he thinks it will give him the 'position of a gentleman.' There is the barrister, the heir to a good estate, who attaches himself to one of the Inns of Court, not with any intention of practising, but because a study of the law will be of service to him when he takes his seat amongst his brother magistrates. And there is the barrister who commands a large business in the lower walks of his profession, who is not held in much esteem by his fellows of the long robe, and who has as much chance of obtaining 'silk' or of being raised to the bench as a bottle of Tarragon vinegar has of developing into '47 port.

To this last class belongs Bob Royston. One of the results of his appearing in the character of the people's friend, and of posing as the enemy of the privileged classes, was gradually to turn his business from the civil into the criminal channel. Many barristers have begun at the Old Bailey, and have ended as the most respectable of Westminster Hall. Royston has reversed the process. He made his name at Westminster, and he is now one of the pillars of the criminal law east of Temple Bar. In all cases where the proletariat have struggled against their masters, or rank or wealth has been guilty of misconduct, he is engaged as counsel

—in the first instance to defend the poor, in the second to expose the rich. Is a tenant of a small holding at war with his powerful landlord, the Agricultural Union comes to the defence, and Royston enters the arena of justice as the peasant's friend. Is a sailor unjustly treated by his captain on a long voyage, Royston is just the man to deal with the case, and to attribute all the blame to the commander and none to the hand. Is labour fighting against the compromises of capital, Royston is the upholder of trades-unionism, and bids the working man not yield a jot of his demands. Is the directorate of a bank accused of defrauding its shareholders, and of robbing the widow and the fatherless, who more severe against a grasping and unscrupulous plutocracy than Royston? Has a wild Irishman been imprisoned for treasonable practices, who can better defend him than the turbulent demagogue? In all election disputes, how scathing are the comments of Royston upon the bribery and corruption practised by the rich! To hear him, one would think that honour, virtue, patriotism, and fair dealing were only on the side of the lower orders.

Royston is an excellent type of the Old Bailey lawyer of the last generation. He has a power of coarse eloquence; a bullying manner of cross-examination; a loud overbearing voice; a face capable of all the expressions of scorn, hate, contempt, and ridicule, which would have made him the bosom friend of Judge Jeffreys. Witnesses have fainted in the box at the mere look of the man. Judges stand somewhat in awe of him, and dislike differing from him or interrupting him,

Jurymen have been days before the sounds of his grating boisterous voice have ceased to buzz in their ears. The fellow knows his power, and does not scruple to use it. Fear him, and he will domineer over you to the last; but brave his furious glances, meet him as he meets you, show him that you are not to be intimidated, and he will cringe and fawn and be as submissive as a whipped hound. Still it must be admitted that it is only a few who are prepared to oppose him. It is not given to everybody to possess the peculiar qualities which subdue the bully, though no man yields sooner than he.

The aim of Royston, like that of most men who live by agitation, is to enter Parliament; but as yet he has been uniformly unsuccessful. In spite of the eulogiums of his newspapers, of the efforts of his itinerant lecturers, and of his obtruding himself, whenever an occasion offers, as the working man's candidate, he has never yet headed the poll. Why he should have been so systematically rejected, it is difficult for me to understand. He is the friend of the working man; the working man pays all his election expenses; the working man quotes him as an infallible authority; the working man adds largely to the agitator's income by paying him to serve on committees and to look after his interests; yet Royston has stood for boroughs where the votes of the working classes should have carried the day, but has not been elected. His political principles are elastic enough for any shire or borough in the country. He is an independent Liberal, or, in other words, inde-

pendent of his party when it declines to do anything for him, but dependent enough when he fancies he perceives rewards in the distance.

It is amusing to watch Royston shift and veer and trim his sails to catch every breeze that blows from high quarters, when he thinks he has the chance of being appointed a judge of county courts, or of conquering the prejudices of the Lord Chancellor against admitting him within the bar. Royston is a very clever man, well read in law, and enjoys the reputation, among certain classes, of being a sound Protestant, a great philanthropist, and a perfect Cato where loyalty to his principles is concerned; yet I should be very sorry to place much faith either in his honour or integrity where a conflict had to ensue between his principles and his interests. The latter, I think, would win easily, and there would be little market for the former. Still, profession is a great thing. People are too indolent or too timid to judge for themselves, and to have the courage of their opinions; and hence, what a man calls himself, the world generally ends by accepting and acknowledging. Royston is the working man's friend, though it seems to me, considering the amount of business the working man brings to Royston, the name is somewhat of a misnomer; it is the working man who is the friend of the agitator, not the agitator who is the friend of the working man.

THE END.

www.ingramcontent.com/pod-product-compliance
Lightning Source LLC
Chambersburg PA
CBHW020323240426
43673CB00039B/896